The

Welborn Families

of the
Old Granville Region
of
North Carolina

A Study of the Multiple Welborns
Living in the
Northern North Carolina Counties
before 1850

Paul Rowland Julian

HERITAGE BOOKS
2016

HERITAGE BOOKS

AN IMPRINT OF HERITAGE BOOKS, INC.

Books, CDs, and more—Worldwide

For our listing of thousands of titles see our website
at
www.HeritageBooks.com

Published 2016 by
HERITAGE BOOKS, INC.
Publishing Division
5810 Ruatan Street
Berwyn Heights, Md. 20740

Heritage Books by the author:

Sorting Out the Early Julian / Juliens:
A History of the 18th and 19th Century Founding Families with the
Surnames Julian, Julien, and St. Julien

The Welborn Families of the Old Granville Region of North Carolina:
A Study of the Multiple Welborns Living in the Northern
North Carolina Counties before 1850

International Standard Book Numbers
Paperbound: 978-0-7884-5715-9
Clothbound: 978-0-7884-6454-6

Acknowledgments

This   work would not have been possible without the availability of the resources of The North Carolina Department of Archives and History; The Randolph County (NC) Historical Society; The Library of Congress; The Clayton Library of The Houston Public Library System, and the commercial on-line genealogical data-bases.

In addition, special mention of local county library staff needs made. In a   few important instances they contributed facsimile copies of critically-important documents quickly and cheerfully.

One of the great failings when
we first undertake to trace our
ancestry is to assume a connection
with a family of similar or
identical surname. This is an
especially dangerous procedure, for
until we develop the ability to
analyze the evidence at our disposal
and to deduce conclusions, based
upon the preponderance of the
evidence, we find ourselves annexing
ancestors who do not belong to us.
Milton Rubincam

PREFACE

This study was prompted by the search for the parents of my
paternal great-great grandmother Elizabeth Welborn. We know she
was born in Randolph County, North Carolina in 1804, was married
in 1826 to my g-g-grandfather Isaac Julian, and journeyed to Indiana
with Isaac. However, owing to the lack of the 1820 Randolph
County Federal census schedule, she cannot be located at age 16–
the 1810 census contains multiple possibilities.

Spurring my interest was the discovery of four John
Welborns in the Randolph County 1810 schedule, two of whom
might have been Elizabeth's father. Four Johns W-s in the same
county! – albeit with slightly different surname spellings, something
not unexpected at the time.

In researching this problem, I discovered that the Old
Granville District contained a surprising number of residents with

the various Welborn spellings. Further, using the published material, and especially the family history sheets posted on the Web, it became clear that descendants of the early 18th century Welborn residents were frequently confused– the same individual being assigned to a different line (or lines) of family members.

The surname with the variable spellings was a common one in 18th Century America, with the result that those residing in the Old Granville District represented only some fraction of the total population.

Thus, I set out to try to place the very early (1750-1800) North Carolina Welborns into distinct families. This does not mean that those early progenitors might not have been related. My goal is simply to organize the available material to ascertain if the various Welborns could not be assigned, uniquely, to definite family groups.

But, it does mean that some expected information might be missing or incomplete, viz, multi-generation family trees. This work, then, represents a somewhat different approach than the family-tree-oriented genealogies– what might be called 'vertical' ones. As the emphasis here is multi-family, we can use the term 'horizontal'.

The reader should not expect complete early three-generation genealogies in all cases. The number of individuals for which some records exist and are included here (~320) precludes such completeness. However, to repeat, the primary objective here is to establish the number of distinct families and their early lineage, assigning like-named Welborns to the correct family.

Hopefully, the contents will help resolve some of the current confusion of the genealogy of this relatively common North Carolina surname. The Family distinctions made herein are the result of about nine years of ongoing data collection; and innumerable creating, discarding, and recreating hypotheses.

In any study this broad there are gaps and uncertain family connections. I have indicated such in the text by the use of _underlined italics._

Any comment on material and Family makeup would be appreciated.

Paul R. Julian
Alexandria VA

TABLE OF CONTENTS

LIST OF TABLES

LIST OF CHARTS

INTRODUCTION

Plan of the Book and Directions for the Reader
The purpose & objectives.

As stated in the Preface, the primary purpose of this volume is to distinguish the multiple Welborns arriving in the Old Granville District before 1800 and to assign the Christian-named descendants to their proper Families.. The reader should not expect a complete three-generation genealogy; but that, insofar as possible, the correct descendants be assigned to their respective families.

Many of the Family members did not remain in the Granville District but moved on to the South and West. In general, Generation 2 (sons & daughters of the original Old Granville Progenitor) & Generation 3 relationships & genealogies for these emigrants are not all treated here, aside from ascertaining to which Family they belonged and the destination of their emigration.

The Old Granville District was one of the first large land areas open to immigrants from the North. As such, it attracted a large number of them; but many apparently saw the opportunity as temporary, or as a way-station on their way South or West.

The Plan of the Book

The approach herein might, at first, seem to put the conclusions or answers first, rather than initially solving the various naming and Family puzzles. This choice was dictated by the inter-connected and multiply-named Welborns with the result that the various Families frequently had to considered simultaneously. The structure of the Chapters is such that a 'back-and-forth' thread is necessary to detail how the puzzles were approached.

In Chapter One the separate Families are set out, with some basic indications given (Progenitor, locations, e.g.) that help distinguish them. In succeeding Chapters, the research undertaken to assign same given-or- Christian names to each of the Families is presented.

Finally, a summary Chapter is given for each of the Families with some detail, if necessary, to emphasize the unique attributes found for them.

Appended, is a (partial) formal genealogy that includes those Family members for which the records and research provided some degree of certainty: it is important to understand that the given formal genealogies are generally not complete, and may include just two (early) generations.

Some conventions and abbreviations

To save repetition on referring to census data, the following shorthand is adapted. Enclosed brackets will specify the Population Schedule of the year indicated. e.g. [1790], the first U.S. Federal census; [1850] the Schedule of the Seventh Federal census, etc.

As the spelling of the early Welborn surnames comprised a rich variety, (sometimes varying in the same document), the text will use 'W-s' when referring to the complex of spellings. However, insofar as possible, the original spelling will be used when reference is to a document or indexed reference. As the decades passed, a gradual settling on the "Welborn" name evolved. Only a single Family eventually consistently used the "Wellborn" spelling.

'Family' with a upper case F will specifically refer to one of the Families treated.
'bible' with lower case b refers to Family bibles.
'Will' with upper case W will refer to same of the Families.

b	born
Co	county
comp	compiler
d or dcd	deceased

d o b	date of birth
fide	source attributed to.... Used here to indicate acceptance of a source not seen.
im	image
m	married or marriage
mfilm	microfilm, generally of FamilySearch.org
m i	middle initial
ff	forward
pps	more than a few pages
/s/	document signed
vol or v	volume
>	greater than / after
<	less than / before
Sr & Jr	in running text only
DAR	Daughters of The American Revolution
FHL	Family History Library, Salt Lake City
GPC	Genealogical Publishing Comp., Baltimore MD
LOC	Library of Congress
MARS	Manuscript and Archive Reference System (NCDAH)
NARA	National Archives & Records Administration
NCDAH	North Carolina Department of Archives & History
NGS	National Genealogical Society
NCGSJ	The North Carolina Genealogical Society Journal
RCGJ	The Randolph County Genealogical Journal
RCHS	Rowan County Historical Society (publication- *The Rowan County Register.*)

Both FamilySearch.org and Ancestry.com archive contributed information from various sources. The former uses 'Family Tree' & the latter 'Public Member contributions'. These are not always unique as some appear both places. In order to save having to sort these out, the book will combine them into 'FamilyTree'.

CHAPTER ONE

THE FAMILIES

Before starting, it is prudent to set out an arbitrary generation chart. Most of the Families studied were traced to the mid-18th century with a clustering of vital record dates (either documented or estimated). The succeeding generations then followed with expected clustering– limited here, however, to just four.

Anticipating the results a bit, seven distinct early (<1770) families could be identified. This is not to say that some of these may not have been related at some early level– indeed we know that two of the early immigrants (Progenitors) were brothers.

These Families all entered North Carolina in the middle-to-late 18th century in lands primarily granted to them in the Old Granville District. Thus, the focus is on the region that was to become Orange, Guilford, Rowan, Randolph, Surry, and Wilkes Counties.

TABLE ONE [1]

TIME SPAN FOR THE ARBITRARY GENERATION
DESIGNATIONS

	Born	Deceased
Generation 1	1730-1740	1780-1810
Generation 2	1755-1770	1825-1855
Generation 3	1777-1815	1874-
Generation 4	1800- 1830	various

The sources used here are the conventional census, land, court, & will records, supplemented by Family bible sources. The latter, while not considered as reliable as the aforementioned,

---

[1] These limits are based on actual or calculated vital data– they are to be used as guidelines for placing members into or in distinguishing generations.

proved to be very good here when cross-checked with other sources.

The various families deemed to be distinct as a result of the study are given an arbitrary alphabetic designation– the order is some what arbitrary and depends, more-or-less, on the amount of material available and the apparent ease of reconstructing the early family history. The designation convention used throughout will be e.g. ThomasA1 indicating Generation 1, Family A; JohnD3, of Generation 3, Family D.

TABLE TWO
FAMILY SUMMARY TABLE [2]
The Old Granville District

Progenitor	Original location	1st Records	Emigrants to
A THOMAS c1735-1778	Sandy Creek	1756 petition 1761 land	SC GA
B JAMES 1737-1811	Abbott's Creek	1759 land 1762 land	SC KY IN MO
C WILLIAM 1733-1792	Sandy Creek	1756 petition 1758 court	GA AL
D JOHN* 1754-1805	Sandy Creek	1773 debtor 1776 marriage	KY OH IN
E EDWARD c1735-1806	Sandy Creek	1756 court 1761 land	KY
F ISAAC 1732- c1800	Grassy Creek	1755 tax 1760 land	---
G JOHN* c1763 - ?	Wilkes County	1796 VA?? 1810 census	---

* Placed in Generation 2- Table One.

---

[2] The seven listed here comprise the main body of the Book: a possible eighth is included in Chapter Four.

The documentation for the records in the Table is given here, and annotated, rather than in Footnotes.

A- Thomas Welborn, 2/10/1761 225A Orange County, Sandy Run, witness- Willam Welborn. Deed Book 12, item 2273. Margaret M. Hofmann, The Granville District of North Carolina, 1784-1763, vol 2 (note the occurrence of William as a witness– there is a problem as to which Wm was involved.)

B- James Wilborne, 10/5/1762 323A Rowan County, Abbotts Creek, adjacent Moses Teague. Patent Book 4?, item 4961. Margaret M. Hofmann, The Granville District of North Carolina, 1784-1763, vol 3.

C- William Willborn, 1761 375A Orange County, S108.947; MARS 12.14.95.267. Also in Bailey, Pat Shaw, Land Grants Records of North Carolina, vol 1, Orange County 1752-1885. Pub. by author, Graham N.C., 1990.

D- John Welborn, the only sure reference to Family D John is the marriage record in 1776. It is possible he was on the debtor list of John McGee's Ordinary. See Chapter Two, Part 1 on the problem of multiple Johns.

E- Edward Wellborn, 30/6/1762 425A Orange County, Sandy Creek, adjacent York. Chain carriers William & Thomas Welborn Patent Book 12, item 2259. Margaret M. Hofmann, The Granville District of North Carolina, 1784-1763, vol 2. Note: this combination of W-s is most important. It suggests that the three were friends if not relatives. It also places the three along Sandy Creek, which together with one-or-more Johns indicates an early land settlement local for a number of the W-s.

F- Isaac Welbourn, 12/10/1760 158A Rowan County, no location.

Deed Book 4, pps 327-9. Jo White Linn, Minutes of the Court of Common Pleas and Quarter Sessions, 1753-1762, vol 1, II:300. There is some question as to the location of Isaac's land. The original land & tax records are   for Rowan Co. but with no watershed information. After the creation of Surry Co. in 1770, the records shift to that county with one location specified, viz Greasey or Greasy Branch. Such a watercourse does not exist today, and a possible interpretation of the name is 'Grassy': such a Creek does exist close to the then Surry-Guilford line, today's Surry-Stokes boundary.[3]

G- John Wellborn, This Family were late-comers to the Granville District. The first records were [1810], [1820]. See Chapter G.

---

[3] This & subsequent references to locations are in The North Carolina Atlas & Gazetteer, 2nd Edition, 1993. DeLorme Mapping, Freeport ME. This location, if correct, is found on p16, panel C2.

The Old Granville District

The history of land acquisition in the Granville District is of interest, although it may not have any direct bearing on the distinction of the various Families. A most comprehensive treatise of this history is a contribution by E. Merton Coulter, published in 1913.[4] His essay is heavily dependent (as it should be) on the Colonial Records of North Carolina, but supplemented by early historical works. Two principal items may be mentioned here as potentially important. First, the chronological dates: in 1744 John Lord Carteret, the Earl of Granville, had his share of the initial Lords Proprietors' grant from the Crown formally approved. The area, known subsequently as the 'Granville District' was surveyed and commissioners appointed.

In 1748, the Assembly passed an act the all land transfers by sales or will be recorded or registered in the appropriate county Court House. Thus, in the chronology of land grants made by the Welborns we expect any grant to be after 1748. Second, in his essay, Coulter sets out the confused situation in land acquisition caused by the fact that Granville's land grants were under his (or his son's) or his agents control with no control by the Crown or the Colony. This situation was further aggravated by the dishonesty and fraudulent behavior of the agents that resulted in conflicting and erroneous grants. The trouble that this situation caused, Coulter suggests, contributed to the Regulator movement.

As a consequence, the tracing of land acquisition & grants might be expected to be difficult, especially considering the evolution of the Counties.

Additional information on land acquisition in the 18th Century may be found in the compilations by Margaret Hofmann

---

[4] The Granville District. The James Sprunt Historical Publications, The North Carolina Historical Society, vol 13, no 1. Durham, 1913

and the Chapter of Lands in Leary .[5] Hofmann's compilations reveal an interesting point: all of the early Family Land Grants were from The Earl of Granville and none from the governor and council under the Lords Proprietors of Carolina.

The Family Locations.

About 1760, Welborn families, as well as the McGees, Teagues, Yorks, Julians, etc, began acquiring lands in the Granville District. The warrant dates and the survey dates were typically one-to-three years apart.

The earliest date found for the W-s that gave an identifiable location was 1756. This was contained in the 1771 petition mentioning that Thomas Welborn lived on (or near) Sandy Creek, Orange County.[6] The locations– Sandy Creek, Sandy Run, Bush Creek are in northeastern present Randolph County and are in land acquisition records for various W-s from 1756 through 1790 (and beyond). Slightly to the west (but distinguishable in the Family records) were the locales of Muddy Creek and waters of the Deep River.[7]

The history of these locations places them in Orange County until 1770-1771 when Guilford County was formed, and subsequently (1779) Randolph County. Between the 1756 date and 1790, Thomas, William, John, and Edward (Family progenitors

---

[5] Leary, Helen F. M., ed., North Carolina Research. 2nd ed., N.C. Genealogical Society, Raleigh, 1996, & e.g. Hofmann, Margaret E., Abstracts of Land Patents, the Colony of North Carolina, 1735-1775. 2 vols, by author, 1982.

[6] This & subsequent land records may duplicate records pertaining to Table Two, pps 3-4.
Colonial Records of North Carolina, vol 9, pp 25-26.

[7] Sandy Creek, DeLorme Atlas North Carolina, p 37, frame 1-B,C.   Muddy Creek, DeLorme p37, frame 6-B,C.

all, with various spellings) received grants at Sandy Creek and immediate environs.

In 1758, Isaac Welbourn was a grantee of land transfer in Rowan County. This record does not reveal the location as did neither the 1759 & 1761 tax records.[8] It was not until 1762 (from the records used herein) that a specific location– Abbotts Creek–was mentioned. Subsequent land records for this location are reasonably plentiful. Today, Abbotts Creek and its tributary Spurgeon Creek are located in extreme northeast Davidson County.[9]

The Sandy Creek and the Abbotts Creek regions are about 22 miles apart, the Muddy Creek region a bit closer.

Other early (1778) grants were to [a] John and Edward in Granville County at Ledge of Rocks and Nap of Reeds locations. Thomas Wilburn, Dutch District, Granville County who signed the Oath as well.[10] In the same year, a Joshua and a John Welborn acquired land in Guilford County very near the Randolph County line.[11]

About 1784, Isaac & William acquired land in the Grassy

---

[8] Not clear is the record of an Isaac in 1759 Rowan County–the record appears in a curious collection in the present Rowan County Library and is, apparently, the origin of the C. Ratcliff reference, v2. p220 as a tax record.

Ratcliff, Clarence E., North Carolina Taxpayers, 2 vols. GPC, 1987-1989.

[9] DeLorme North Carolina Atlas, p 37 , frame 5B.

[10] These names & locations are from The Colonial Records of North Carolina, v22, p179 recording the taking of an Oath. DeLorme North Carolina Atlas, p20, frame D1.

[11] Map by F. Hughes, published by Guilford Co. Genealogical Society. Original references are not given & no records of these lands have been found in County records.

Branch drainage of present Surry County, hard by the Stokes County line..[12]

TABLE THREE
OLD GRANVILLE LOCATION TABLE

Water Course	Present County	Families	DeLorme Atlas
Sandy Creek[13]	Randolph	A, C, D	p37, 1-B,C
Muddy Creek Uwharie Riv.	Randolph	A	p37, 6-B,C
McEntyres Creek[14]	Randolph	C	p 38, 1- C
Abbotts Creek	Davidson	B, E	p37, 5-B
Ledge of Rocks[15]	Granville	E	p 20, 1, D
Nap of Reeds	Granville	E	p 20, 1, D
Grassy Creek	Surry	C	p 16, 1- 2,C
Mitchell River	Surry	C, F, G	p 15, 6-B,C
Grassy Fork Swan Creek	Wilkes	F	p 15, 5-6, D

---

[12] DeLorme NC Atlas, p16, panel 1-2C.

[13] Also recorded as Deep River

[14] MARS : 12.12.68.3

[15] MARS : 12.14.66.1753

Noted here, importantly, there are records other than land grant or deed transfer records that can establish residency in a location. Chief among these are court, petition, and will records. For example, we can place an Edward Wilborn in Rowan County in 1754– he was appointed as constable. In 1771, Thomas Wilburn/Welborn signed a petition in Orange County to be pardoned as a Regulator. [16]

Particularly important in locating the early Welborns are petitions for various relief or for new counties. In 1771, 1779, 1780 signed petitions locate the following: Thomas, 1771 in Orange Co. (Sandy Creek); William (Jr.!) Orange Co. (Sandy Creek) in the same petition locating them both in place in 1756. John in 1771 in favor of John Pugh (also Wm /s/) In 1779, John, Thomas, William signed and in 1780 Thomas. Most of these were pleas for new counties or administrative centers.[17]

A summary of the Tax, Petition, and other important lists is given in Appendix Three.

A document of some importance in locating early settlers in the Old Granville District is contained in the estate papers of Col. John McGee, Orange County, circa 1773. This is a list of debtors to the McGee estate and contains a number of residents as customers to John McGee's Ordinary.   A tabulation of surnames in that list is instructive, indicating family concentrations in the region. There

---

[16] Linn, Jo White, Abstracts of the Minutes of The Court of Common Pleas and Quarter Sessions 1753-1762, vol 1, pub by author, 1977, p33 from Court II:59.

MARS: 308.11.2; also see Records of The Executive Council, p678.

[17] 1779 Guilford Co., petition for a new County. NCGSJ 38(2), p140-1. /s/ by William, John, Joshua, Thomas, & Caleb, Fam A.

were 6 Allreds [var], 6 Clarks, 7 Jacksons, 6 Julens (Julians), 7 Lambs, 8 Morgans, 6 Smiths, 6 Welborns [var], & 8 Yorks.] [18]

> Of possible demographic interest, there are 543 names on the debtor list. Of these, thirty-one were women: 19 couples, 7 widows, & 5 apparently unattached

The Problem of duplicate given names.

.   To attempt to sort out all these land records vis a vis the various Welborn families, we note that as families migrated to new locations they tended to stay near one-another. As a research strategy, then, a first cut at attempting to separate the new Old Granville families is to assume that at each location, above, individual Family groups were concentrated.

In Table Two we included only those Welborns who belonged to Generation 1– The Progenitors. The problem of name duplication for Generation 2 and 3 is a major problem treated in Chapter Two in Parts. To emphasize this, all of the Families had in Generations 2 & 3 Williams. Six had Johns; Five had Isaacs, and Four had Samuels.

It is, of course, possible that some of the duplicate given names are of the same person. However, as above, the first step is to assume that these are different individuals and look for further strategies to conclude otherwise. As example: there are records for Edwards in 1754 and 1756 in Rowan; in 1761 in Orange County; and in 1771 in Granville County. After the two very early records, a gap of 15 years occurs before the Granville/Orange records. Do these apply to the same individual? See Chapter Three, Family E.

For the Isaacs, records in 1755 & 1758 in Rowan and 1758

---

[18]   A complete list of the debtors can be found in The NCGSJ vol 1(1), p38ff.

in Orange seem to point to two different immigrants.

Williams appeared in 1756 and 1761 in Orange County; 1758 in Rowan; and 1773 in Guilford. (=Orange?). A few of these records are appended with the indication of a "Sr" and "Jr". These appellations need not indicate a father-son relationship as, in early days, they also could indicate simply "older-younger".

As noted, Chapter Three includes a formal genealogy for those Family members for which the records and research provided some degree of certainty: it is important to understand that the given formal genealogies are probably not complete, and may include just two (early) generations.

Websters New Encyclopedic Dictionary, Merriam-Webster, Springfield MS, 2002.

parsing (transitive verb) 2: to examine in a minute way: analyze critically.

Used here, parsing will refer to analysis of the census age bracketing in an effort to establish Family lineages. For example: if an [1800] for a Family member enrolled 3 males under age 10; using all records it might be possible to identify those sons by name. And when a widower remarries a widow, it is possible that she brought some of her own children to the marriage. Parsing successive census may verify this event.

This procedure must be used with care– Ancestry's FamilyTree contributions provide examples of erroneous associations using 'census surfing' to find a fit. When used here, the identifications will be supported by census, Family bible, court, and deed information.

CHAPTER TWO

THE DUPLICATE GIVEN NAMES

CHAPTER TWO
Part One- The John W-s

Of all the multiple W- given names encountered, John presents the most complicated task of assigning them to the correct Families. Not only is the number of individual Johns at issue, confidently equating the documentation and reference citations to the proper John is a problem. We note that six of the seven Families included at least one of the name.

CHART OF JOHNS

	Location	Reference support
A2	Ra- SC?	bible, divorce
B2	Ro	marriage, burial
D2	Ra	Progenitor
E2	Or	Will
F2	Su, St	Estate
G2	Wi	Progenitor
A3	Ra	Rev., bible, m2
B3	Ro	burial
D3	Ra- IN	in Will, own Will
G3	Wi	

Key- Or Orange; Ra Randolph; Ro Rowan; Wi Wilkes; Su Surry; St Stokes

All have census support.

Part One- The Johns of Granville, Orange, Guilford, & Randolph Counties.

The method used here of separating and assigning the various Johns to the correct Family depends upon sequential steps:

• The [1790 & 1800] for Hillsboro District, & Orange, & Randolph Counties.

• The Family bible entries.

• Parsing the census age distributions to compare with the bible entries.

There are three [1790], two in Hillsboro and one in Orange County. First, for age distribution 1/4/5 and nearby Esther 1/-/2: second for distribution 1/3/5; and for Orange the ages are lacking. In [1800], two– one in Randolph County near a Jean W- with a distribution 3 - 2 - 1 / - 2 - 1 - ; the other in Orange County enrolling a couple both b<1755, with no children.[1]

The Family bible entries list three Johns as Family Head: two Generation 2 & a single 3. There is, apparently, no Family listed there that upon further investigation could have been located in Orange County. (See below)

Next we look for bible data that indicate that one of the two Randolph County Johns had four sons b 1774-1790, and the

---

[1]   U.S. census.

1790 Hillsboro District NC, John Wilburn household. Roll 7, p284, line 25, (im 167).

1790 Hillsboro District NC, John Wilborn household. Roll 7, p282, line 1 (im 166).

1790 Orange Co., John Wilbern. Given as Roll 7, p63 which is erroneous. The publication of The First Census of The United States 1790, GPO 1973 p96 gives John Wilburn, St Mary's District Orange Co. with no distribution. This is presumably from a tax list as the original census was lost.

1800 Randolph Co., NC, John W- household. Roll 32, p347, line 20. Also Jean W- household. R32, p347, line 11.

1800 Orange Co., NC, John Welborn household. Roll 41, p 601, line 3.

other three. The number of females is the same in both. The only information that the [1800] provides is for one Family, with three males (<10) b1790-1800; and two 1774-1784.[2]

This parsing results in : John A2 (1/4/5) with sons John, Joseph, William L. & Elisha and females Esther, Martha, Nancy, ?, and wife Mary. This result is reinforced by the census listing near Esther W- that land records make clear was the wife (and relict) of Progenitor Thomas- Table Two.[3]

For the John in [1790] with 1/3/5, the bible includes an entry with children Jesse Y, Elias, William and Anna, Elizabeth, Martha, Sarah, and wife Sarah Y(ork). The bible also includes a John (Jr.) b 1790 and two other sons born later & not in the census. See Chapter Three, Family D.

For the [1800], both John A2 & his wife Jane née McGee were in census separately & would divorce. When we examine the two [1800] the age distributions to account for the division of the children, the effort seems fruitless. The story of this event is told in Chapter Three, Family A.

There are a few records that can reinforce the separation of the two Johns above.

The 1785 tax list from Randolph Co. contains two or three John W-s: Capt John Welborn's District has a John taxed on 895A along Sandy Creek and (another) 200A in Guilford Co. in the Stinking Creek Quarter. Neighbors here include 5 Hinshaws, 3

---

[2]   Genealogical data from bibles in the possession of The North Carolina Historical Commission. Transcribed by The North Carolina DAR. Family History Library Catalog, FHL US/CAN Film 18067, item 3. N.B. this reference will occur frequently in this book & subsequently will be noted as FHL US/CAN Film 18067.

[3]   Easther (sic) 1779 tax record Randolph Co. Ratcliff, Clarence E., North Carolina Taxpayers, v 1, p217. GPC, 1987-1989.
     U.S. census. 1790, Randolph Co. NC, Esther Wilbern household, Roll 7, p 284. Age distribution 1/-/2 & next to John.

Lambs, & a single Julen (sic).

In Robert McLain's District, a John Welborn, 235A was listed, but with no drainage indicated. Neighbors here include 7 Allreds, 5 Yorks, 5 Handshaws (sic), 4 Julians, & 3 Trogdons.

The interpretation here is that the two are different taxing (or militia) districts that contain different Johns with quite different neighbors.

As there are no records specifying (in 1785) the exact locations of the militia & taxing Districts, we resort to the watershed information given in Table Three, p 9. Here we can distinguish between the Sandy & Muddy Creek drainage, and from above assign John D2 to the former & John A2 to the latter.

A full discussion of this choice is given in the respective Chapter Three Family précis.

The reader should recall the statements made about the iterative nature of the research method employed. The number of Families and individuals considered is so large that Family distinctions demanded, after all records were collected, a back-and-forth assembly & decision making procedure.

Thus, it may seem the assignments above arbitrary– but they are the result of those iterations.

At this point only information before 1810 has been analyzed. The reason for this is clear when [1810] is encountered.

Table Four
1810 Federal Census Randolph County[4]

		< 10	10-15	16-25	26-44	> 45	< 10	10-15	16-25	26-44	>45
1	John Wilbourn				1		1			1	
2	John Welbourne	1			1		2			1	
3	John Wilborn	1				1	2			1	
4	John Wilborn	2			1		2			1	

A number of conclusions are evident:

1- one of the Johns, #3, is older than the others: from Table One probably in Generation 2.

2- the distribution of family members is different for all.

3- the fact that the Schedule is listed in alphabetic fashion (by surname) would seem to indicate that no information on locations or neighbors can be had– but see below.[5]

---

[4] U.S. census, all 1810 Randolph Co. NC
John Wilbourn household, Roll 38 p 213(57), line 13.
John Welbourne household, Roll 38, p214(58), line 15.
John Wilborn household, Roll 38, p 216(60), line 8.
John Wilborn household, Roll38, p 216, line 11.

[5] Even with an alphabetic listing the #3 John occurs next to a Jean = Jane his estranged wife.

In an investigation, a detailed examination of all 57 pages of the Schedule was carried out. The family names Allred, Hoover, Welborn, & York were tallied– these families are known to be residents of the Sandy & Muddy Creeks region of Randolph Co. All consisted of groups listed (on different pages) with intervening different surnames. This can be interpreted to indicate that the final Schedule was pieced together from different lists, presumably of local militia units. None of the individuals, moreover, was duplicated from group-to-group leading to the conclusion that no Family was enrolled twice.

It is thus apparent we are dealing with four different Johns. Consideration of the sex and age distributions and the Family bible information from above, we may assign #3 in the Table to John A2. In similar fashion, #2 is identified as John A3. (See Chapter Three Family A for the issue of this John and their d o bs.)

Most importantly, we are left with two individuals in the same age class, b 1765-1784. One has no male issue and one female <10; the other two males <10 and two females <10. A very important problem in untangling the John W-s is the proper identification of these two, if possible.

Number 4 in the [1810] Table has two sons less than 10, but the 'father' age 26-44 cannot be D2 as he was deceased in 1805.

As the [1820] for Randolph Co. is missing no help from that census is possible. There are two tax lists for Randolph County– 1815 & 1820, however that must serve as proxy for the missing [1820]. There are just two Johns included in the 1815, & 1820 records and the information given is not sufficient to assign the one or two (if different) to any particular Family.[6]

Thus, we are presented with a puzzling dilemma– there are two Johns identified in the [1810] Randolph County & the analysis above as A2 & D2; only one certain in [1800], and in 1815 & 1820 either one or two that could well have been the aforementioned . And leaving the two unidentified in [1810] to somehow be accounted for.

---

[6] Hinshaw, Winford C., 1815 Tax List of Randolph County, N. C.. WPJ Genealogical Publications, Raleigh 1957.

Grigg, Barbara N. & Carolyn N. Hager, 1820 Tax List, Randolph County North Carolina. Randolph County Historical Society, Asheboro, 1978.

One possibility is afforded by the Family bible entry for John D3, born in December of 1790.[7] This John is listed as an orphan in the 1808 estate of his father attaining his majority in 1808-1813. (See Chapter Three, Part D.)

An additional record is of a marriage of John Welborn to Barbary [sic] Brower in July of 1809, time enough for the couple to have had a baby girl.[8] This suggests the possibility that #1 of the Table is John D3. The age may be a problem– the age class is 1765-1784– but given the age problems of the early census, this evidence may be provisional. If, indeed, John D3 was b 1790, then he would have been 18 or 19 at the time of the Brower marriage and age 20 for the [1810].

In any case, assignment of one of the Johns as D3, leaves the other, #4, above with two young sons, as unknown.

The remaining John W-s outside of the Sandy-Muddy Creeks region of Randolph County are as follows:

The Orange County schedule is lost, but a John is credited with a land grant in 1796. Additional Orange/Granville land records place a John in the Ledge of Rocks, Nap of Reeds region. [9] The land was apparently very close to the Granville/Orange County line (as it was then– see the location discussion in Chapter One.) This border location was distinct from the Sandy Creek location.

This John is identified here as John E2, son of Edward. Both

---

[7] Family History Library Catalog , FHL US/CAN Film 18067, item 3.

[8] NC marriage record 01 289 NCSA, Raleigh.

[9] Land records Granville/Orange Cos.: 1778 140A Ledge of Rocks, MARS 12.14.66.1753; 1795 Camp Creek, MARS 12.14.95.2257 & 2386; 1796 grant Nap of Reeds, MARS12.14.95.2257. The same year John was a grantee of 200A on the Orange-Granville line in Deed Book 5, folio 628.

took an Oath in 1778 in the Nap of Reeds District.[10]

• Summing up the somewhat involved considerations above, we can confidently place Family A, with **John A2 & A3** in the Muddy Creek region of Randolph County. The **Family D** John is located in the Sandy Creek region of present north-eastern Randolph County. And **John E2** remains somewhat geographically separate in Orange County.

Part Two- The Johns of Rowan County.
The Rowan County records provide evidence for two Johns that are associated with the Abbotts Creek region– today's Davidson County. Family B, is distinctly of Rowan County and the Johns are certainly of that Family. But this large & complicated Family has more than its share of genealogical problems.

With Progenitor James' Will and deed of land records involving the Family eight sons, in toto, are clearly indicated– but no John.[11] A son, Joshua, appears only in the Will.

Two records point to a Generation 2 Family B John: an 1802 marriage to Lydia Teague and a burial record, both in the Abbotts Creek area.[12]

---

[10]   The Colonial Records of North Carolina, v22, p179.

[11]   Linn, Jo White, Rowan County Deed Abstracts, vol 1 1762-1772; Pub. by author, 1983, p111. The abstract is from Deed Book 7: folio 357 (July 1771) & lists as grantees the brothers Moses, Aaron, William, James, Isaac, Gideon, & Samuel.
          Progenitor James' Will (text) is in Peden, Eva Coe, comp., Barren Kentucky Will Book No. 1, pub. by Charles Peden, Glasgow KY, 1979, p 33. (Feb. 1811). Only sons Samuel, Joshua, & Gideon are mentioned.

[12]   Marriage record from N.C. Register of Deeds 022 3304. Burial in Abbotts Creek Primitive Baptist Church.

As no John was evident in James' documentation– footnote 11– we parse the census.

For James B1 [1790, 1800, both Rowan Co.; 1810 Barren Co. KY]. [1790] had 2/3/4 giving James & another b <1775; 3 between 1774 & 1790 suggesting John 1786, Samuel c1774, & Joshua 1780. (sons Isaac, William, Gideon, Aaron, & James (jr) had their own census.) Incorporating [1800], one 10-16 must be John b1786 & one 16-26 must be Joshua– consistent with [1790].

The parsing, thus, gives evidence of eight sons. In [1810] only a 16-25 (1784-1794) remains, again John b1786. If this analysis above is correct, James' son John (B2) was the last born of the eight sons (rather an afterthought as Joshua, the next youngest, was b 1780).

John had a son **JohnB3** after his marriage to Lydia Teague in 1802. This son was buried as John T. M., b 1820 & d 1874. No record of a marriage has been found. [13]

A second **John B3** was the son of Joshua (of the Will) who traveled with his father & grandfather to KY. He appears in [1840, 1850, & 1860] in Monroe Cos. KY & IN. [14] In the former, he is listed

---

Findagrave #77333504, with photo of stone. Dates b 1786 d 1824. Lydia's grave is nearby.

[13] Findagrave # 15403932, Abbotts Creek Primitive Baptist Church Cemetery, plot left row lot 9– next to Lydia lot 10. Photo stone. Dates Oct. 12, 1820, Feb. 23, 1874.

[14] U.S. census
1840 Monroe Co., KY, John Wellborn household, R120, p 253, lines 8-10. Next to Joshua & Mary Ann.
1850 Monroe County, IN. John Welborn household, R161, p 338.
1860 Monroe Co., IN. John Welborn household, R282, p 610, family 589.

next to Joshua. In the latter two, the age given has him b 1798 and a wife Mary b NC in 1794.

The distinct Johns, above, of Family B appear to be in satisfactory shape. However, in terms of the overall problem of Family Johns, there is more to consider. Complicating matters, a 1792 Rowan Co. petition was signed by four (or five as there was a James Jr.) of the seven sons of James B1, plus a John. As this John must have been of age to sign, assuming no deliberate malfeasance, he must have been b c1774. In 1815, Johns Jr & Sr were taxed.[15]

Here there is little doubt that the Jr & Sr refer to different unrelated individuals as John B2 b1786 would have been only 29, the inference is that the Sr was older. However, no other Rowan County John appears in any record found! Any explanation of this 'extra' John is in the realm of speculation. There were the two Randolph Co Johns of the [1810] (as above) unaccounted for, and it is possible that one of them had records in both Counties. Abbotts Creek and the Muddy Creek of Randolph Co. are only a few miles apart. (See p 7)

Part Three- The Johns of Surry, Stokes & Wilkes Counties.
Family F is defined by a series of records in Wilkes & Stokes Counties. The Progenitor Isaac left an estate, filed in 1800, that listed his heirs one of whom was **JohnF2**. [16]

---

[15] The Rowan County Register, #13, issue 1, p2908. The petition was for a "Seperate Ellection" for a County militia unit.
Linn, Jo White, (The) 1815 Rowan County, North Carolina, Tax List. By author, Salisbury, NC, 1987. In Capt. Wilbourn's Compy: Wilbourne, John Jr. One white poll on 154A; Wilborn, John Sr. One white poll, no acreage, both p30.

[16] A facsimile copy of the very brief estate record is in the author's collection– very kindly sent by the Staff of the Stokes County Library. The only record of Isaacs' son John is
U.S. census
1800, Stokes Co. NC, John Wilborn household. R32, p 613, line 10.

Family G was a late-comer to the Old Granville Region, arriving about 1797. The Progenitor, another John, was b in VA <1765. Two sons accompanied him and two more were b after 1797, providing the estimate of the Families' arrival in Wilkes Co. Son **John Jr** was b 1806 and lived past 1860, all in Wilkes Co. He was enrolled in the [1840, 1850, & 1860] Wilkes. These gave his d o b and his wife as Martha .[17]

Conclusions for the Family assignments of the multiple John W-s.

The five Generation 2 Johns in the Chart can be rather confidently separated as the records make clear. Only Family C did not name a John in any generation treated here.

Johns A2 & D2 are proven distinct by many records; and B2 by virtue of County location and a burial record. **John E2** was located in the eastern-most region of The Old Granville District and left a Will. **Family F's John** was listed in his father' estate.

Generation 3, however, is different in that although five Johns can be identified as to Family, there are two that cannot. This seems a challenge for future research, but one that will require more records than have been examined in this Book.

One would like more records from the western-most Counties as a complete Generation 3 for Families F & G is difficult to establish.

He was credited with two young daughters & no sons.

[17]   U. S. Census Wilkes Co NC
1840, John Wellborn household. Roll 373, p74(28), line 6th from bottom.
1850, John Wellborn household. Roll 649, p278B, family 408. From the household list there is evidence of a split family or boarders from a neighboring Pearson family.
1860, John Welborn household. Roll 918, p 77, family 1090. John b1806, wife Martha b 1813, & 3 sons & 6 daughters listed.

CHAPTER TWO
Part Two, The William W-s

This duplicate name appears in four Generation 2 and in six Generation 3 Families. The number of documented Williams in Guilford and/or Randolph Counties requires some attention (Chapter Four).

CHART OF WILLIAMS- Three Generations

	Location History	Reference support
C1	Ra- Wi- GA	Will, bible. Progenitor
A2	Ra SC	land records
B2	Ro	Will, bible
C2	Ra	petitio, military
F2	Su-St	heir in Estate
A3	Ra	abundant records
B3	SC (MO)	in Will of father (MO)
B3	KY	census Family association
B3	*KY*	*parse*
C3	Wi-TN-MS	in bible & Will
C3	*GA*	single record, Family location
D3	Ra	in Will, bible
E3	KY	census Family association
F3	*Su-St*	*parse*

Key- Ra *Randolph*; Ro *Rowan*; Wi *Wilkes*; Su *Surry*; St *Stokes*

Using records from the Family bibles, tax & petitions, and deed & land records; a number of Generation 2 Williams can be identified. Particularly confusing are the 1773 & 1779 petitions from Guilford County that contain, inter alia, two William juner.[sic]; and (a plain) William twice.[18] A detailed comparison of these signers indicates that different groups of, presumably, neighbors or militia districts signed each. The six year gap between the two petitions has been the subject of an article explaining the difficulties surrounding the establishment of Randolph County.[19]

In 1785, the Randolph County tax list recorded no Williams, but Ratcliff reported one in 1779 presumably from a tax record.[20] Apparently early taxing procedures were not always complete or records are lost. The early land records, before 1779, were in Orange Co. in the Sandy Creek region. Families A, C, & D all had land in the Sandy Creek & Muddy Creek region.

With this situation, the procedure here follows that of the previous Part: we take all the Williams from the will, bible & census data, and seek to bolster the separations these provide with deed & land records.

---

[18] In 1773, two William jrs occur & a single [plain] Wm.: in 1779 a single Wm is listed. These petitions requested that Guilford County be split, forming Randolph Co. to be.

[19] See RCGJ III(3), p78-9 for article by Mac Whatley (Lowell McKay Jr).

[20] 1785 Tax List, RCGJ II(1), 36-45 & II(2), 18-27 (1978). List taken by C. R. Briles from Randolph Co. records.
    Ratcliff, Clarence E., North Carolina Taxpayers, 2 vols. GPC, 1987-1989. 1779 from v1, p217.

Generation 2

William (A2). His father's (Thomas) 1778 Will specifies the last seven sons as minors– William is the last of the list suggesting he was the youngest– a d.o.b range of 1760 to 1777 (assuming 18 was the age of majority).[21] The NC [1790], however, does not enroll him; and it appears he migrated to SC along with his siblings. There, in Union County, he was enrolled in [1800 & 1810]. Using the two census age classes, his d.o.b. is 1774 (assuming the age class assignments are accurate) well within the range above. His subsequent history is a task for SC researchers.[22]

Family **B2- William**, son of James, B1, Rowan County. b 1761, d 1828, well documented. He stayed his entire life in Rowan County. The Family bible record is detailed and is supported from other documentation. His Will was probated in 1842 & burial was in Davidson Co.[23]

William C2 is identified by only two records. He is listed among the sons of his father included in the Roster of Revolution Soldiers of Georgia (where William C1 had gone in the mid-1770s.) In a pre-Federal census work in GA, both a William Sr & Jr were

---

[21] A copy of this Will is in the author's archives: from Guilford Co. Book A, p400ff.

[22] U.S. census
1800 Union County SC, William Wilburn. Roll 50, p 223, line 4. (A young couple, near siblings Elijah, Epheraim, & Joshua).
1810 Union County SC, William Wilborn. Roll 61,p 582, line 7. (Issue). He does not appear in [1820].

[23] Will Book 6-folio 116 & Findagrave # 17625909, Spring Hill Cemetery both Davidson Co.

taxed in Wilkes Co..[24] There are, apparently, no subsequent certain records.

William F2 is clearly distinguished as he is listed in the Estate of his father Isaac.[25] Both were residents of Stokes Co.

Generation 3

William A3, son of John A2, left a long series of records in Randolph County including a marriage record, tax, & court records. As a consequence he is easily distinguished from other Williams. See Chapter Three, Family A for citations.

In Family C, a Generation 3 **William**, son of James, did not remain long in NC, but removed to TN & MS. In some citations he is referred to as William Wilkes, pointing to his origin in Wilkes County NC. The Family bible includes him as William Wilkes, although he is not an heir in his father's (James) 1853 Will. He married Ann Perkins about 1823. Both are buried Benton Co. MS.[26]

---

[24]   McCall, Mrs. Howard H., comp, Roster of The Revolutionary Soldiers of Georgia, v1, p177 (original 1941) Clearfield reprint, 1996. This author gives b 1733 in NC- White, V.D.'s Genealogical Abstracts, National Historical Publishing Co., Waynesboro TN, 1992 gives #3731, p 50 as b VA.
            Hudson, Frank P., A 1790 Census of Wilkes County Georgia from tax returns, The Reprint Co., Spartenburg, 1988. p 76. The other names on the page are all Family C members.

[25]   A copy of the Estate facsimile is in the author's possession. The source is the Stokes County Library staff.

[26]   U.S. census
1840 Shelby Co., TN. William Wellborn household. Roll 350, p 211, line 11th from bottom. Age class 40-49.
1850 Marshall Co., MS. William W. Wellborn household. Roll 377,

A second Family **C3 William** is identified by Wilkes County GA records including an early tax record.[27] At present, there is no clear evidence of his parentage other than his location with the Family C in GA where his father William resided (above).

There are records that distinguish two Generation 3 Family B Williams: by a Will record & census. **William** of James Jr appears in the latter's St Francois, MO Will, although he remained in SC.[28]

A William appears in a Schuyler Co., MO [1860], b 1805 in KY. As both his father & grandfather were resident there, it appears that this William may, indeed, be a B3.

Joshua's son **WilliamB3** spent most of his life in Monroe County KY, appearing in two Family census, & moving on his own across the border to TN. [29]

---

p31, family 442.
   Findagrave, Franklin Family Cemetery, Benton Co., MS.
William W., # 37114578– b 11/1799 d 11/ 1864.
Ann Perry Franklin #37114498– b 1804 d 1884.

[27] Early GA records Davidson or Lucas?
   U.S. census 1820, Wilkes Co., GA, William Wilbourn household. Roll 8, p 151, line 20. Age class 1795-1804.

[28] Abstracts of Wills, Bonds, & Adms., 1822-1852. Welborn, James – Will dated 15 July 1841. St. Francois , Missouri records. Fide Mountain Press, Signal Mountain, TN, 2006, p22. Heirs included.

[29] U.S. census
1810 Monroe Co., KY, Joshua Wilbourn household. Roll 5, p 46, lines 16-19. A Family group.
1820 Monroe Co., KY, Joshua Welborn household. Roll 25, p 205, lines 10-12.
1830 Overton Co., TN, William Welbourn household. Roll 179, p 176, line 6.
1840 Overton Co., TN, William Wilborn household. Roll 533, p 34, line 10. Throughout, his age class is 1790-1800.

A provisional *William*, located in the same KY County as his presumed father Gideon, is included by a parsing.

William D3 was of the Family that remained in Randolph County– the son of Progenitor John (Table One, Chapter One) Both the Family bible and his father's Will record him. [30]

William E3 is included based on three KY census in association with his 1st cousin Edward. (See Chapter Three, Family E.)

A *William F3* is included from a parsing of his father Samuel's census.

---

[30]   U.S. census, Randolph Co., NC
1800, William Wilborn household. Roll 32, p 351. Young couple.
1830, William Wilborn household. Roll 125, p 63, line 4.
1850, William Welborn household. Roll 641, p 226B, family 942.
b1778NC.
        1803 tax record, Randolph Co. RCGJ II(1), p 6

CHAPTER TWO
Part Three- The Isaac W-s

The given name Isaac was one of a number of biblical names (some others; e.g. Moses, Elijah, Ezekiel) used by the W- Families of Generations 1 to 3. The other names were all after English Royalty, with the interesting absence of George.

CHART OF ISAACS- Three Generations

	Location History	Reference Support
F1	Ro- St	Estate, burial
B2	Ro- KY	deeds, petition
C2	Or- GA- AL	military
F2	Wi- Su	Estate
B3	Da	m i P, in Will, marriage
B3	MO	biography
C3	TN	see below
D3	Ra-	bible, Estate
F3	Wi	marriage

Key- Ra Randolph; Ro Rowan; Da Davidson; Or Orange; Su Surry   All have census support.

Generation 2

B2 Isaac, the son of James, was b c1760 and d 1824. He is listed on a 1771 deed record of his father together with his siblings.

In 1791 a grantee of land from his father.[31] He moved sometime about 1800 to Barren County, KY along with James and brothers Samuel, Joshua, & Gideon. He appears in Barren Co [1810], but not in [1820], and does not appear in James' 1811 Will.[32] According to a St Francois Co. MO document (see below) he moved to that County in 1818 and d there in 1824 intestate.[33]

C2   Isaac was b 1758 in NC (County?) and d 1839 in Madison County AL. His essential records appear in White's Abstracts of the Revolutionary Pensions Files. Burial was in the Hazel Green Cemetery in Madison County AL. He was designated as a DAR Patriot, survived by his wife Mary née Barton. [34]

---

[31]   Grantee from his father James, 50A Abbotts Creek. Kluttz, James W., Abstracts of Deed Books Rowan County, North Carolina. Book 13 (1791), #2518, p 912.

[32]   U.S. census 1810 Barren Co. KY includes the Family group of James, Sr; Samuel, Joshua, Gideon, James Jr. R5 p45, lines 16-19. Isaac is listed on previous p 46. (For James' Will see Chapter Three.)

[33]   Saint Francois County, Missouri Records, pub by Mountain Press, Signal Mountain TN, 2006, p22. The cited record is from Abstracts of Wills, Bonds, & Adms. 1822-1852.

[34]   Service was in both GA & AL. White, Virgil D., Genealogical Abstracts of the Revolutionary War Pension Files, Vol III. National Historical Publishing Co., Waynesboro TN, 1992, p 3736.
    Isaac applied for a Pension in 1833 leading to the record cited. Burial record from Hatcher, Patricia Law, Abstract of graves of revolutionary patriots. Heritage Books, Westminster, MD. 2007 ed., vol 4, p172.
    DAR, Patriot Index volume III, Gateway Press, 2003, p2887.

F2 Isaac is potentially confused with F1 his father. The Family was located in Rowan County, and later in Surry & Stokes Counties when they were formed. A Findagrave record lists Isaac F1 as d c1800 and buried in The Abbott's Creek Primitive Baptist Cemetery. No stone is included, but attached material refers to a Stokes County Estate, listing his heirs.[35] In [1790] Isaac, presumably Sr, is credited with four adult male (b <1775), two males b 1775-1790, and five females.[36] This is obviously a family group– and we may speculate that the assemblage is Isaac Sr with three sons. The sons listed on the Estate record are William, Isaac, John, Samuel, James, & Daniel. See Chapter Three, Family F for details & Family History.

Separating F1, F2, & B2 Isaacs requires some attention as all three were in Rowan Co at the same time. Separation of the Generation 2 Isaacs of Families B & F is afforded by the sequence of land & deed transfer records in Rowan & Surry Cos during the years 1787-1789. These are distinguished by the locations identified– Abbotts Creek of Rowan Co (for Family B) & the Greasey or Grasy Branch of the Surry Co Yadkin River (DeLorme Atlas, p16, panel 2C), for Family F. Note: these all were recorded in a two-year span.[37]

---

[35] Findagrave record # 68312432.   A facsimile copy of the estate record supplied to the author by Library of Stokes County.

[36] U.S. census, 1790 North Carolina, Salisbury (Rowan), Isaac Wilborn Sr. Roll 7, p 322, 3rd line from bottom. Alphabetic listing

[37] 1787 Isaac. Rowan Co; land entry 45A Abbotts Creek. Pruitt, A.C., Abstracts of Land Entries 1778-1795, #3098. MARSid 12.14.107.2798 Warrant for 46A in Back Bay of Abbotts Creek. (This is probably the same parcel.)
1789 Grantee Isaac Wilborn, ".... son of James Wilborn for 5 sh, 50A on Abbotts Crk adj Phillip Mock's stillhouse and James Wilborn's homestead. Sd land was part of a State grant to this {William Davis} Grantor. " Wit: William Welborn, James Wilborn. Kluttz, James,

Generation 3

B3 Isaac, son of William(1761-c1828) of Family B. Isaac occasionally used middle initial 'P' [38]. Born in 1822 he nevertheless is in Generation 3. William's second marriage was in 1807, and Isaac was the last of his children as mentioned in the 1842 Will of his father.

See Chapter Three Family B for details of this complicated Family.

B3 Isaac, son of Isaac, b 1806 d>1889 . In [1810] he was in Barren Co KY (but not in [1820]). A St. Francois County MO biography includes a history of a Welborn family comprising Isaac (Sr), and his son Isaac, b about 1806, and married to a Ms Jemima Matkin. The [1860] for St Francois, MO provides confirming evidence for Isaac & Jemima. [39]

Rowan County Deed Abstracts, Abstracts of Deed Books 11-14, 1786-1797, pub Landis NC, 1996. From Deed Book 14, 2588 p 14, 13 Jan 1789. p129.

1789 Isaac, State Grant #1814 of 200A, Grasy Branch, Sibeden Fork (of Yadkin R.), 18/5/1789. Kluttz, James series, Deed Books 11-14, Book 14, 987. On same date, Isaac (x) Wilburn of Surry Co deeds to William Wilburn of Stokes Co 200A Greasey Branch, Wachovia Line, being the State grant to Isaac; Kluttz same reference # 2351. The speculation here is that Progenitor Isaac Sr is deeding his new land to his eldest son. See Chapter Three, Family F.

[38] U.S. census, 1850 Guilford Co. N.C. Isaac Wellborn household. Roll 632, p 262B, family 14. (This [1850] includes NC County of birth– age 25 Davidson)

Findagrave # 17625952, photo of stone has initial 'P'.

[39] Saint Francois County, Missouri History and Biographies, pub by Mountain Press, Signal Mountain TN, 2006. p81. This reference is a copy of a work published in about 1889 (from the dates included in the text) that Mountain Press does not explicitly acknowledge– while

C3 Isaac, son of C2 (above), The connection to his father, rather tenuous, is given by the [1850] in Shelby County, TN listing him, age 67 (1783) born NC, and living with a William Allen, age 20 b AL.[40] The connection with Isaac C2 who was in NC in 1783 & shortly thereafter in AL (above) is inferred by his companion b AL. For [1850], we have census for D3 in TN below and [1860] for B3 above, effecting the separation

D3 Isaac, son of D2 John, traveled about a bit. He was in [1830] Posey County, IN and in [1850] Obion County, TN. The probate of the estate of his father listed devisees Isaac, John, Enoch, and Elizabeth. The Family appears in the North Carolina Family Bible records. Isaac's d o b is given as November of 1793, and the entry notes that he moved to TN. [41]

F3 Isaac, was in [1830] Wilkes Co NC, b 1800-1810; with a marriage record, 1828, to Elvira Tomlinson. The assignment of his parents depends upon the marriage record and parsing of the census for the Family. The marriage bond posted was by S. Welborn. Parsing reveals a single F2 member with an age class to accommodate

---

providing information one wishes for better documentation.
U.S. census, 1860 St Francois, MO, Isaac Welborn household. Roll 654, p 134, family 657.

[40] U.S. census, 1850 Shelby Co. Tennessee, Isaac Wilburn household. Roll 895, p204, family 1788.

[41] U.S. census
1830 Posey Co IN, Isaac Welborn household. Roll 29, p 172, line 20. 1850 Obion Co TN, Isaac Willburn household. Roll 891, p 347B, index reads as 'Millburn'.
Will John Welborn, Randolph Co. Will Book 3, pps 27-29.
Family History Library Catalog , FHL US/CAN Film 18067, item 3, p 171.

a 1800-1810 birth: Samuel F2– in both the [1810 & 1820] Isaac, however, apparently did not live much past 1830 as Elvira was enrolled in [1840].[42]

---

[42]   U.S. census
1830 Wilkes Co. NC, Isaac Wellborn household. Roll 125, p 394, line 1.
1810 Wilkes Co. NC, Samuel Wellborn household. Roll 43, p 273, line 18.
1820 Wilkes Co. NC, Samuel Wellborn household. Roll 83, p 376, line 3rd from bottom.
1840 Wilkes Co., Kilbys Dist., Elvira Wellborn household. Roll 55, p373, line 4th from bottom. A young widow.
        Marriage Wilkes Co. NC, 7 Feb 1828, Isaac Wellborn & Elvira Tomlinson, bond S. Wellborn. From County Court Records-FHL #0546475-81. In North Carolina Marriage Collection 1741-2004, available on Ancestry.com.

CHAPTER TWO
Part Three, The James W-s

CHART OF JAMESES- Three Generations

	Location History	Reference Support
B1	Ro- KY	Will, burial
B2	Ro- SC, MO	deed, Will
C2	Wi	bible, Will, marriages
F2	Wi	occupation, Will
B3	?- MO	in Will
B3	Da	bible, marriage
B3	KY	census Family association
B3	GA	census Family association
C3	Or- GA,AL	census
C3	Wi	bible only (b 1808, d-1827)
C3	*GA*	*Findagrave*
D3	Ra	bible only d @ age 15.
E3	TN, KY	census Family association
F3	Wi	in Will

Key- DA Davidson, Or Orange, Ra Randolph, Ro Rowan, Wi-Wilkes

The Progenitor James left many records, including land in both Rowan & Randolph Counties. He moved c1810 to Barren County KY, leaving a Will in 1811. See Chapter Three, Family B.

Generation 2

Separating the Welborns with the James given name requires some effort to insure that the records available do pertain to that Family complex.

The **James Welborn B1** had a son, **James**, b 1764, & d 1841 in St Francois MO. Son James is not mentioned in the 1811 Will: the link must be established by a deed in 1771/2 listing the sons of James, Sr.[43] He moved, along with his brothers, to SC and thence to MO leaving a Will in 1841.[44]

N.B. Likely confused with James B1 in the KY records is the occurrence of a Col James W- (various spellings in seven records) resident in Muhlenberg County KY from 1771 until 1826. The names of most of his children do not fit the NC Family names, and there is no evidence he ever resided in NC. In many FamilyTree records, his family is connected to this Book's Families.

---

[43] Linn, Jo White, Rowan County Deed Abstracts, vol 2 1753-1762. Pub by author, typescript, no date, p133. (Available e.g. Clayton Library, Houston TX.)

[44] U.S. census
1800 Pendleton Co SC, James Wilburn household. Roll 50, p159, line 17. (Near brother Aaron).
1810 Pendleton Co SC James Wilburn household. Roll 61, p252/262, line 20. (next to brother Moses).
     Will abstract; fide Saint Francois, MO-Records. Mountain Press, Signal Mountain TN, 2006, p22. Source is W&B: 90-92/ A:51. The heirs are listed.

James Wellborn, C2, b 1767, d 1854 was the son of C1 William; the Family principally of Wilkes County NC. He is included in the Family bible records, with a fairly complete dossier. A second marriage, however, does not appear there. The [1850 Wilkes Co.] gives his age as 82, with wife Rebecca– both his two wives carried that name.[45] A distinguished politician, he was a member of the NC Senate variously from 1796 through 1835. His Will was dated 27 May 1853 [46] See Chapter Three, Family C .

He must, moreover, be distinguished from the following James as both left records in Wilkes County; which family, however, requires special consideration. Census in1850 show a James Welborn, b 1778 in Rowan County– in the [1820 Wilkes Co. NC] as well as [1830 & 1840 & 1860] his occupation is sometimes given as Blacksmith, with the age group consistent with a d o b of 1778. [47] His wife was named Rebecca, but no marriage record has been found.

---

[45] U.S. census. James was enrolled in every Wilkes Co. census from [1800 to 1860], surely something of a record. They will not be listed here– any census program can recover them.

Marriage record. James Wellborn to Rebecca Johnson, 1813 in Wilkes Co. NC marriage bonds 02 259.

[46] Rowan Co. Register, vol 7 #3 (1992) p 1602. Probated Jan. of 1855, heirs listed. See also MARS 5200.104.696.

[47]   U.S. census, all Wilkes Co., NC
1820 James Welborn household. Roll 83, p 506, line 4th
 from bottom: the income/job query at the end of the Co. listing gives his occupation as blacksmith.
1830 James Wilbern household. Roll 125, p 372, line 11.
1840 James jr Wellborn. Roll 373, p 58, line 19. (Next to Daniel).
1850 James Wellborn household. Roll 649, p 363, no family given.
His d o b 1778 in Rowan Co. The occupation is not readable, but does not appear to be blacksmith.

The 1871 Will is in Will Book 6, folio 32. Mitchell, Thornton W., North Carolina Wills: A Testator Index,1665-1900. Corrected & revised edition, GPC, Baltimore, 1993.

Estate proceedings in 1800 Stokes County list this James as a son of Isaac Wilborn, born in MD about 1732. Such would assign **James** a label as **F2**.[48]

Generation 3

James B3. The only certain record of this James is as an heir of his father James– recorded in the state of MO in 1841.[49] He apparently was not with his father at the time as no MO [1840] can be found. His presence elsewhere remains unknown, although a possibility is the James b 1784 who left [1820 through 1850] in GA counties.

James B3, son of Aaron b1784, [1840, 1850] in Jackson Co GA. He parses along with his siblings Aaron jr, Elisha, & Thomas.[50]

Another Family B3 was **James M**. (presumably Madison), the son of John, b 1812. The Family bible includes him, and a marriage record exists. All census enroll him as James M.[51]

---

[48] Findagrave #68312432, listing the heirs of Isaac F1. This added information is taken from the Facsimile footnote # 42 or 51.

[49] Saint Francois County, Missouri Records,, pub by Mountain Press, Signal Mountain TN, 2006. p22. The original cited is WB: 90-92/A:51.

[50] U.S. census, Jackson Co GA
1840 James Wilburn household. Roll 44, p30, lines 19-22. Family w/Aaron, Gideon, William, presumably sons.
1850 James Wilbiorn household. Roll 74, p26B, family 387.

[51] U.S. census, Davidson Co. NC
1840, James M. Willborn household. Roll 259, p 264, line 2.
1850, James M. Wellborn family 107, Roll 652, p 229.
Marriage to Sarah Horney; NC marriages 03 742, NCSA.

Finally, a ***James B3*** is included based upon location with his father Samuel, & a supporting parsing of KY census. See p88, Chapter Three.

James C3, was the son of Isaac, b Orange Co. NC, who moved c1790 to GA & Madison Co. AL. The link is established by a Family grouping in [1830, 1840], with father Isaac, & siblings Elias and Isaac Jr. [52]

Another **James C3**, son of James, lived 1808 to 1827. Listed in the Family bible as James Johnson with a newspaper death notice in November of 1827. [53]

Finally, ***James Madison Welborn, C3***, son of Elias. His history is found in a Findagrave of his father, including a biography. The link from father to son, James Madison, is attributed to DAR records.

James D3, also died young. The Family bible lists him simply as d @ age 15

James F3, son of James, b 1828, was listed as heir in his father's Will. In [1880] his Family was included next to his

---

[52]   U.S. census, Madison Co. AL
1830, James Welbourne household. Roll 4, p 79, line 15. (d o b 1780-90).
1840, James Welborn household. Roll 13, p 119, line 20. (Same d o b & p as James Sr, Jr & Elias).

[53]   Broughton, Carrie, L. comp., Marriage and Death Notices in Raleigh Register and North Carolina State Gazette 1826-1845. GPC, Baltimore, 1975, p306.

brother Daniel.[54]

---

[54]   U. S. census
1880 Wilkes Co NC, James Willborn household. Roll 987, p126A,
Families 45, 46. Next to Daniel.

CHAPTER TWO
Part Five, the Thomas W-s.

CHART OF THOMASES- Three Generations

	Location History	Reference Support
A1	Or-	bible, Will, deeds
A2	Gu- GA	in Will
E2	Gr- KY	petition, Will
B3	SC- IL	of Wm census only
B3	SC	of Aaron's Will
B3	MO	of JamesB2 in father's Will
F3	Wi	burial record

Key- Or Orange, Gu Guilford, Gr Granville, Wi Wilkes
All have census support

    Progenitor Thomas arrived in the Sandy Creek area prior to 1761; was a Regulator; and left a Will in 1778.[55] The Will lists his children with two sons, John & Joshua, and a list of 'not of age' that included Thomas. As a minor he must have been born after 1760.

    Progenitor Edward's 1806 Surry Co.Will, (E1), includes heir Thomas E2.[56]

---

[55] As regulator, Colonial Records vol X pps 560,761, 826.
Will Book A/folio 400- author has copy.
Land, Sandy Run S108.253, MARS 12.13.10.2273.

[56] Book3: folio 71. Author has copy.

Generation 2

The separation of the two Generation 2 of this given name–
A2 & E2 can, in addition, can be done on the basis of location.
Family A's earliest land holdings were in the Sandy Creek region
and Family E in the Dutch District of Granville Co [57].

Thomas, E2, son of Edward left records in NC & KY. Most
of his NC records are listed in Granville County (The Dutch District)
whilst those of his father are in Orange County. A 1780 Granville
petition in favor of one John Hampton was signed by Thomas. There
is no NC [1790] for any Thomas. The First Census of Kentucky,
however, locates a Thomas in 1790 in Madison County along with
his brother Zachary; and in [1810] in Cumberland County KY. In
1791 a marriage record to Sarah Gerrard is reported in US &
International Marriage Records (Ancestry.com) with no supporting
evidence. In 1816 a Will was filed in Cumberland County. [58]

A2 Thomas, b c1758, d 1826 in GA. There are few clearly
identifiable records for this Thomas in the Family location of
Guilford/Randolph Counties. A military record from the

---

[57] Register, Alvaretta, K., State Census of North Carolina. 2nd
ed. revised, GPC date?– 1784 Dutch District 'census' with 1/5/3.

1779 petition for dividing Guilford to create Randolph
County, RCGJ XXXV(4), p50-1.

1780 listed in Capt. John Hinds Company, Revolutioary
War (with brother Joshua), RCGJ XXXI(3), p21-2.

[58] Petition: Series: North Carolina General Assembly Box:
Aug-Sep 1780 NCSA; accessed Ancestry.com Jan 2014. Note; this is
the same year Thomas A2 was in the NC militia-below.

First Census of Kentucky, 1790. Heinemann, Charles B.,
GPC, 1966, p100.

U.S. census 1810, Cumberland Co., KY, Thomas Wilbourn
household. Roll 9, p 706, line 14.

Will Index v II 1815-1840, Book B (no p), Feb 1816.
Ancestry.com FamilyTree ref., content shown.

Revolutionary War places Thomas in a 1780 Company of John Hinds.[59]. Thomas moved to GA acquiring Bounty Land in 1784. Early GA records thereafter are from a variety of sources. In1790 e.g. in Wilkes County GA a land transaction occurred in association Thomas' siblings Ephreim, Joshua, & William. The DAR gives a birth date of 1760, & date of death of 1826 along with a record of two wives & issue.[60]

E2 Thomas moved from The Dutch District to Cumberland Co KY, leaving a Will in 1816.[61]

Generation 3

The name in Family B becomes relatively common in this Generation: three cousins can easily be identified.

Thomas, son of Aaron, b July of 1789; m Mary Polly Martin 1810 in Anderson District SC; d Aug 1868 , with a Will &

---

[59] Revolutionary War: RCGJ XXXI(3), p21-2. The 1779 petition from Guilford County signed by a Thomas (and also by his brother Caleb), RCGJ XXXV(4), p50-1.

[60] Bockstruck, Lloyd D., Revolutionary War Bounty Land Grants, GPC, 1998, p562.
Tax Lists 1794,1796, Wilkes Co. GA, Blair, Ruth, Some Early Tax Digests of Georgia. GA Dept. Archives & History, 1926-reprint 1971. Pps 292, 296.
De Lamar, Marie & Elizabeth Rothstein, The Reconstructed 1790 Census of Georgia. GPC, Balt., 1985.
McCall, Mrs Howard H.,comp, Roster of The Revolutionary Soldiers in Georgia, v II, Clearfield reprint (1941), 1996, p126.

[61] King, J.E.S., Early Kentucky Wills. Reprint GPC 1969 [1933]. Will Index, v2 1815-1820, Book B, no p#.

buried in that County.[62]

Thomas, son of William (and Rachel, William's 2nd wife) has bible support indicating that he removed to IL about 1830. Indeed, he can be found in that State in [1840] and in a state census in 1855.[63] He was born c1808, late for Generation 3, but was of William's second marriage.

Thomas, son of James B2 was in his father's MO Will, and in the [1830 & 1850] in St Francois.[64] The latter gives his d o b as

---

[62] Findagrave #s 9696919 & for Mary #9696933. There is a very modern stone for Thomas, but an original recognizable one for Mary. "Polly Wife of T Welborn...."

Will probate Aug 1868 in Pendleton SC. Alexander, V., C.M. Elliott, & B. Willie, Pendleton District and Anderson Counties, South Carolina Wills, Estates, Inventories, Tax and Census records. Southern Historical Press, Easley, 1980, p158..

Thomas W. , wife Mary, sons William, Thomas, Aaron, James. Executors James, Aaron, probate 28/8/1868.
He is inferred to be the son of Aaron B2 owing to a parsing of [1800 & 1810], and his inclusion of a son Aaron as executer.

[63] Family History Library Catalog , FHL US/CAN Film 18067, item 3, p173.

U.S. census, 1840 Cass Co., IL, Thomas Willman (sic) household. Roll 56,p 36, 9th line from bottom. Issue.

Illinois State census, 1855, McDonough Co., Thos J. Welborn household. IL State Archive, Roll 2192, line 3. Accessed Ancestry.com.

[64] Will of James Welborn, St Francois Co., MO, July 1841. St Francois, Missouri County Records, Mountain Press, Signal Mountain MO, 2006, p22.

U.S. census
1830 St Francois, MO, Thomas Welborn household. Roll 72, p 420, line 14. Same p as James, Samuel, & Isaac.
1850 St Francois, MO, Thomas Welborn household. Roll 413, p?, family   .

1803 and a wife Susan.

Thomas F3, son of Daniel, lived in Wilkes Co NC most of his life; moving to TN where he is buried.[65]

---

[65]   Findagrave # 88585202, Washington Co TN.
        U. S. census Wilkes Co NC [1840, 1850, 1860]

CHAPTER TWO
Part Six– the Samuels

CHART- Three Generations

	Location History	Reference Support
B2	Ro	in Will
C2	GA	Will
F2	Wi	in Estate
A3	SC	census only
B3	Ro Gu	bible, burial
_B3_	_KY_	
C3	Wi	biography
C3	GA	estate
F3	Wi	marriage only

Key- Gu Guilford, Ro Rowan, Wi Wilkes

The given name applied to three Generation 2 individuals, easily distinguished:

Samuel B2, son of James b c1756 and mentioned in his father's Will. He moved to KY along with his father & brothers.[66]

---

[66] Will, footnote 59.

Linn, Jo White, Rowan County Deed Abstracts, vol 1 1762-1772; Pub. by author, 1983, p111. The abstract is from Deed Book 7: folio 357 (July 1771) & lists as grantees the brothers Moses, Aaron, William, James, Isaac, Gideon, & Samuel.

U.S. census, 1810 Barren Co., KY, Samuel Wilbourn household. Roll 5, p 75, line 5th from bottom. Next to his father.

Samuel C2, son of William, b 1763. He is not in his father's Will, but is included in the Family bible record. Along with his brothers, he moved to Wilkes County GA leaving a Will in 1822 [67].

Samuel F2, son of Isaac, mentioned in the estate of Isaac, Stokes County. Census for 1810 through 1840 in Wilkes County include him.[68] See Chapter Three, Family F.

Generation 3
Five (Six) Generation 3 Samuels can be distinguished. (There appears to have been no given name Samuel in Families D & E at least in the first three Generations.)

Samuel A3,s only record   found is a census in SC in proximity to his siblings.[69]

---

[67]   Smith, Sarah Quinn, Early Georgia Wills & Settlements of Estates; Wilkes County. Clearfield Pub., 2003 (1959). Listed as a non-cupative Will, p24.

[68]   U.S. census, Wilkes Co., NC
1810, Samuel Wellborn household. Roll 43, p273 (860), line 16.
1820, Samuel Wellborn household. Roll 83, p 376, line 3rd from bottom.
1830, Samuel Willborn household. Roll 125, p 373. Note:
Ancestry.com accessed c2000 showed image 76 as p 372, image 78 as p 375 & no image 77– this may have been fixed since.
1840, Samuel Wellborn household. Roll 108, p 373, line 3rd from bottom.Age 1770-1780 & alone. Note the consistent double l spelling, characteristic of the Family.

[69] U.S. census. 1820 Pendleton Co., SC, Samuel Wilbourne household. Roll 61, p 226, line 3rd from bottom.

Samuel B3's vital data comes from a Findagrave and the Family bible. His records are from Rowan, Davidson, & Guilford Counties.[70]   The Family bible data includes an July 1810 m to Catherine Clinard giving a d o b of December 1795.

A possible *Samuel B3* is suggested by a Rowan [1800] & Cumberland Co KY [1820] Samuels that contain a son in age class 1790-1800. The [1820] in Cumberland Co enrolls what looks like a mixed family that could contain both Samuels. Such speculation results in a hypothetical status for this Generation 3 Samuel.[71]

Family C contributes a third generation **Samuel**, b 1816; son of James (and one of his heirs) & grandfather William. Frequently using his middle initial 'C' (= Chapley), he remained in Wilkes County NC . His death was in 1856 & burial next to his father.[72]

---

[70] Findagrave #17625975, with recognizable stone.
Family History Library Catalog , FHL US/CAN Film 18067, item 3, p54. This bible entry contains his vital data and issue.
U.S. census
1820 Rowan Co NC, Samuel Willburn household. Roll 81, p320.
1830 Davidson Co., NC, Samuel Wilborn household. Roll 120, p246, line4. Age class 1780-1790.
1850 Guilford Co., NC, Samuel Welbourn household. Roll 632, p260B,family 81. b Davidson Co 1791.

[71] U.S. census
1800 Rowan Co., NC, Samuel Wilborn household. Roll 33, p 370, line 9. One son <10.
1810 Barren Co., KY, Samuel Wilbourn household. Roll 5, p 75, line 8th from bottom. One son 1015.
1820 Cumberland Co., KY, Samuel Wilbourn household. Roll 19, p159(136), line 4. Distribution w/ 7 males, 5 females.

[72] Rowan County Register, vol 7, #3, p1602.
U.S. census, 1850, Wilkes Co., NC, Samuel Wellborn household. Roll 649, p 336, line 11. Listed next to his father James, age 82.

Hugh M. & Samuel C. were twins and a product of James 2nd marriage to Rebecca Johnson. (Chapter Two Part C)

The case for a second **C3 Samuel** can be pieced together from the Estate records for Samuel C2 in 1822 & Samuel (jr) in 1827. The elder left a nuncupative Will but with no reference to a son, Samuel. Mary, presumably his wife, was the Estate Administratrix. An entry notes that Samuel paid a debt of Mary's that would seem to confirm the existence of such a son. The [1820] for Samuel (Seml (sic) in Ancestry.com access) indicates at least three sons providing space for Samuel Jr, as well as brothers (no parsing has be done for this occurence.)[73]

Samuel F3. A Wilkes Co. marriage record with Daniel as witness provides the only clue as to his parents. [74]

---

[73] The legal information can be found in Davidson, Grace Gillam, Early Records of Georgia, v2, 1932. Pub. by Rev. Silas Lucas jr., Vidalia Ga. In 1968, p78   &   Smith, Sarah Quinn, Early Georgia Wills & Settlements of Estates; Wilkes County. Clearfield Pub., 2003 (1959), p24.

U. S. census
1820 Wilkes Co GA, Seml (sic) Wellborn household. Roll 9, p 169, line 38.

[74] An 1836 m record to Susanna Deal, FHL 000546481. His brother Daniel was the witness.

CHAPTER THREE
Family Précis & Formal Genealogy

FAMILY A   THOMAS WELBORN Progenitor

Précis.

Generation 1: Thomas' birth date is unknown: he died in 1778 leaving a will.[1] His wife, as heiress, is not named in will, but there are records (see the Formal Genealogy below) that point to Esther Welborn as his wife [2]. Only the eldest son, John 1756-1825, remained in the Granville District, the others moving south to SC GA, & AL. The ten named in the will: John; Ruth ; Joshua ; Cealep (sic) = Caleph ; Thomas ; Ephreim ; Ezekiel ; William ; Eny (sic) =Amy. The last seven were designated as minors– born after 1762.

Generation 2: Eldest son John married Jane McGee, daughter of John McGee of Randolph Co fame–as proprietor of an 'Ordinary' whose patrons included a goodly number of Randolph County early inhabitants (See page 10, Chapter One.)

The marital history of this couple produced some of the more interesting records of Randolph County, indeed of North Carolina, at the time. From these records the attempt to construct the issue of the marriage, and of the extra-marital issue is a difficult, if not an impossible task. Using the census parsing & the Estate record of Jane, some of the issue is fairly firm.

---

[1] The Wilburn book (Wilburn, Hiram C., Welborn-Wilburn History, Genealogy. Micro-reproduction of the original published Waynesville N.C. Miller Printing, Asheville, 1953. Available FHL film 1421486.) says b 1735 with no documentation. This book is not trustworthy, although the d o b seems reasonable. The will in Guilford Co, Book A, p400.

[2] There are multiple records of Esther in Rand Co 1779- 1795, but no maiden name available. Various FamilyTree claims give both Bramer & Esther Robinson/Robertson, with no sources.

Jane McGee was b 1760 of John McGee ?- 1774 and Martha McFarland; d 1/1835.[3]   She married John Welborn in 1776 in Randolph Co . In 1823 Jane filed for divorce.[4] The most important information in the divorce petition is the fact that she states that they separated in 1793: and that she had raised six children *of the marriage* (author's italics). But importantly, she gives no information as to the dates of the six– were they all born <1793?   In fact, including census, estate, and the bible records; there is evidence of nine children & a possible tenth.

In parsing the [1790 & 1800] Randolph Co accounting for the male line seems straightforward, with John, William, Joseph, & Jesse (See below) all in the proper age classes. The female line, though, presents problems. In [1790] one or two cannot be accounted for; although in [1800], Martha, Susannah, & Esther fit into the proper age classes.

At the time of Jane's estate in 1835 she acknowledged four sons and four daughters: the children mentioned explicitly; John, William (noted as deceased), Joseph, Jesse, Patsy Mullen, Esther Hanner, Mary Clark, & Susan Gallimore. This total of eight is to be compared with the six (un-named) Jane specified in the 1823 divorce document.

Considering all of the above, some conclusions are warranted: 1) the marital fidelity of John and Jane is very much at question, and 2) John by 1810 had acquired a sizeable family including a woman

---

[3]   Findagrave # 20774475, with excellent photo of stone. Jane was occasionally known as Jean. In John McGee's Will his daughters are given as Jean, Susanna, & Nancy. North Carolina Genealogical Register, vol 1, p349.

[4]   The text has been printed in various places, including a modern web page. The North Carolina Genealogical Society Journal, vol XXV(3), p323ff reproduces the entire petition. Also see- NC Archives, Public & Private Laws of NC, 1823-26; Chapter CLXI, pps 94-95.

old enough to be another legal wife (no records have been found), or a common-law one, or a live-in companion. None of these could have been of the union of John and Jane McGee Welborn.

The story becomes more interesting when the aforementioned estate records for Jane McGee Welborn are examined. The Estate records are in the NC State Archives (C.R.081.508.144), examined by the author in May 2009.[5] These are filed by surname & consist of court papers , sale of estate items, etc. Most of the documents have to do with the division of slaves. However, most importantly, the proceedings met at the house of Joseph Welborn, & included a petition from Joseph, & Jesse Welborn, & Hugh Mullin [sic] & wife Patsy (=Martha), the eldest daughter according to the bible entry. The Estate records include her as both 'wife Martha' & Patsy, widow.

Included is an astonishing court document relating to the division of slaves. A slave Charles that the executors were recording as not to be sold has the following- " . .. said Charles only for the lifetime of his mother, one Jane Welborn. It is there fore ordered by the court that so much of the order above mentioned made at the Nov term 1832 as related to the sale of the said Charles be rescinded and made void."

The foregoing material illustrates aspects of domestic and marital life in the late 18th century that is rarely documented so completely. The 'dry' bastardy lists of county court proceedings, while of sociological use, can hardly approach the story of John and Jane McGee Welborn. The sensitive subject of illegitimacy is covered in excellent modern fashion by L. Cates in the NCGS Journal, vol 39 (1) 2013 pps 5-34.

Indeed, it may never be possible to identify all of the issue of John & Jane McGee Welborn, together & separately.

.

---

[5] There is a partial record of this Estate file in the RCGJ vii(4) 1983, p37ff.

FORMAL GENEALOGY

Generation 1

1.Thomas Welborn [1], vital data b1735, d 1778; m Esther ?. Will dated 1778. First record in The Old Granville District is 1756 implicit in a 1771 petition; the first (of four) land record was in 1761 in the Sandy Creek region of present Randolph County.[6] The only census record is for Esther in [1790]. Thomas was apparently a Regulator with listings in The Colonial Records.[7]

The children of Thomas [1] & Esther:

+	2	i.	John,	b c1756.
	3	ii.	Ruth	in will
+	4	iii.	Joshua,	b1758.
	5	iv.	Cealep [sic] =Caleph, in will.	
+	6	v.	Thomas	b c1760
+	7	vi.	Ephreim	b?
+	8	vii	Elijah	b?
+	9	viii.	Ezekiel	b?
+	10	ix	William	b?
	11	x	Eny [sic] =Amy, in will. No records.	

The last 7 are designated as minors in the will, b > 1762.

---

[6] Land acquisition 1761; MARS 12.13.103.16 & 12.13.10.2273. (These are also in the M. Hofmann compilations.) The petition, MARS 308.11.1.2.1.

Will is in Guilford Co Book A, folio 400. His wife, included, is not named but his children are.

[7] C.R. vol X, pps 560,761, & 826. Also in NCGJ v3 1977(2), p 78. The petition in 1771 (above) asked for a pardon. The text included the statement that he had been a resident of the Co since 1756.

U.S. census 1790 Randolph Co, NC, Esther Wilburn household. Roll 7, page 284; next to son John.

Generation 2

2. John Welborn [2] **(Thomas** [1] **)** b c1756, d 1825; m Jane McGee 1776, divorced 1823. Spending all but a few years in Randolph Co, his census are [1790] and after the divorce in [1810]. According to Janes's divorce petition they separated in 1793 & she mentioned that he traveled away from the Family. Accordingly he was, almost certainly, in SC in [1800].[8] Chapter Two, Part One presents the difficulties of sorting out the various Randolph Co Johns– there are records that cannot be confidently assigned to this John. No will is known.

Owing to the divorce & the subsequent uncertainty of parentage (as discussed above) the list here includes those in the Family bible & mentioned in Jane's 1835 Estate.

The children of John [2] and Jane

+	12	i.	Martha	b 1777
+	13	ii.	John (Rev.)	b 1779
+	14	iii.	William	b 1785
	15	iv.	Susannah	b 1785 m Jesse Gallimore
+	16	v.	Joseph	b 1790
	17	vi	Esther	b 1793 m James Hanner in in 1802
	18	vii.	Nancy	b ? d 11/1821 m Dougan Clark in 1807. Also as Mary? in Jane's Estate.
+	19	viii.	Jesse	b 1795

---

[8]   Family bible; Family History Library Catalog , FHL US/CAN Film 18067, item 3, pps 173, 198.

U. S. Census
1790 Randolph Co, NC, John Wilburn household. Roll 7,page 284, line 25. Next to Esther.
1800 Union Co, SC, John Wilburn household. Roll 50, page 223, line10. Alone, but near his siblings Ephreim & William.
1810 Randolph Co, NC, John Wilborn household. Roll 38, page 60, line 8. Next to Jean.

20   ix.   Elizabeth b?   m Michael Ramsour
                She appears in the Family bible, but is not
                recognized in Jane's Estate.

4. Joshua [2] **(Thomas** [1]**)** b 1758, d ?   The life of Joshua
was of a man on the move. He was b in Randolph Co, moved
subsequently to GA, SC, & TN. The DAR designated him a Patriot
as a result of service in the Revolutionary War. A brief, but
important biography is in White's Abstracts of the Revolutionary War
Pension Files.[9] This reference gives a d o b of 4/20/1758. Also
included is a record of his moves. Chronologically: a petition in 1779
Guilford Co; deed records in Wilkes Co, GA from 1787 thru 1792;
census from SC [1800 1820 Union Co] & census from TN [1830 &
1840]. He left a will, 1842, in Carroll Co, TN.[10] Note that in the deed
reference his wife appeared as Elizabeth, whilst his will mentions a

---

[9] White, Virgil D., Genealogical Abstracts of the
Revolutionary War Pension Files, Vol III. National Historical
Publishing Co, Waynesboro TN, 1992.
DAR, Patriot Index volume III, Gateway Press, 2003, p2887.

[10] Petition for dividing Guilford & creating Randolph Co,
NCGSJ v38(2), p140-1. This petition was /s/ by five Family A
members.
        Deed (e g) 1790, Wilkes Co, GA. Joshua & Eliz. Grantors to
Sarah Salmoes. Davidson, Grace Gillam, Early Records of Georgia ,v
2, p 124.   Pub. by Rev. Silas Lucas Jr, Vidalia Ga., 1968.
        U. S. Census
1800 Union Co SC, Joshua Wilburn household. Roll 50, page 222, line
4th from bottom.
1820 Union Co SC, Joshua Wilbern household. Roll 121, page 146, 9th
from bottom.
1830 Gibson Co TN, Joshua Wilbourn rersidence. Roll176, p250, line
14.
1840 Carroll Co TN, Joshua Wilborn household. Roll 521, p31, line 16.
        1842 will, Dec term, Carroll Co Court. Text reads wife
Jinsey, sons Thomas, William, Cabel; daughters omitted as heirs. Fide:
Ancestry.com, accessed Dec 2010.

Jinsey. This appears to be, with the lack of any m records, another 'nickname' problem.   Issue.

6. Thomas [2] **(Thomas** [1]**)** b c1758, d 1826, m2. Most of Thomas' records are from the military. The DAR has a Patriot record, as well as a Revolutionary War Bounty Land award. He was a petitioner in Guilford Co, NC in 1779 (ibid). Shortly thereafter he removed to GA with land, tax, & census records.[11]   The DAR reference notes two wives; Sarah née Cloud & Mary née Cooke. He was the executor of his father's will. Issue.

7. Ephreim [2] **(Thomas** [1]**)** b c1760,   d ? Removed to, first, Washington Co, GA; thence to Union Co, SC with his brother Elijah, below.[12]

8. Elijah [2] **(Thomas** [1]**)** b < 1775, d ? Two records in Randolph Co NC, including the [1790]. He moved to Union Co, SC

---

[11]   McCall, Mrs Howard H., Roster of Revolutionary Soldiers in Georgia, v II, GPC, 2004, p126.

DAR Patriot Index, Centennial Edition, Part 3, p 3144.

Listed in Capt. Hinds Company, Revolutionary War. RCGJ xxxi(3), p21-2.

Tax Lists Wilkes Co GA, 1794. Blair, Ruth, Some Early Tax Digests of Georgia. GA Dept. Archives & History, 1926-reprint 1971, pps 292,296. In Franklin Co GA 1806, 1811 in Jackson R. V. Georgia census 1790-1890, accessed Ancestry.com Jan 2011.

[12]   Land record 1784/5, Greene Co GA. L:ucas, Silas Jr, Index to Headrights & Bounty Grants in Georgia 1756-1909, Vidalia SC, 1970, p706.

U.S. census, 1800, Union Co, SC, Ephreim Wilburn household. Roll 60, page 223, line 6. He is missing in subsequent SC census.

with Ephreim. [1800 & 1840 Union Co SC]. FamilyTree gives additional data, undocumented, of a m to Mary Rowntree & to their son Elijah (A3).[13]

9. Ezekiel [2] (Thomas [1])   b ?   d ?   The only record of confidence is the /s/ of the 1788 Randolph Co petition along with brother John. There is a m record in Wilkes Co, GA that may be this Ezekiel (see Ephreim, above).[14]

10. William [2] (Thomas [1]) b c1760, d ?   William was involved in real estate records in Randolph Co from 1784 until 1799 whence he removed to Union Co, SC [1800 & 1810] joining his siblings.[15] His d o b is estimated from the 1784 land patent– if of age

---

[13]   Appointed to jury duty, 1789 in Randolph Co RCGJ xxxiv(4), p 34.
U. S. Census
1790 Hillsborough, Randolph Co, NC, Elijah Wilburn household. Roll 2, p 284.
1800 Union Co, SC, Elijah Wilburn household. Roll 50, page 221, 3rd line from bottom.
1840 Union Co, SC, Elijah Welborn household. Roll 189, page 516, line 11. Age class 60-70 (1770-1780).

[14]   1788 Randolph Co petition, RCGJ III(1), pps29-38. This petition was one of two (1783) asking for a new location for the Court House.
1792 m to Peggy Striblin, Wilkes Co GA. Ancestry.com.

[15]   1778, 150A Sandy Creek , MARS 12.14.103.82. If age 18+, d o b was c1760. 1790 200A Brush Creek, MARS 12.154.103.600.
U.S. census
1800 Union Co, SC, William Wilborn household. Roll 50, page 223, line 4. Ephriem & John (b <1766) same page.
1810 Union Co, SC, William Wilburn household. Roll 61, page 582, line 7. Family group in this census: Wm, John, Ephreim, Joshua,, & Elijah (as above).

(18?) he must have been born about 1760, well within the range of possibilities for his siblings.

Generation 3

12. Martha [3] **(John** [2]**, Thomas** [1]**)** b 2/1777, d 12/1839 m2 to Gilbert Gray & Hugh Mullen. Also known as Patsey e g in Jane's Estate record. Marriage record for Patsey Gray to Hugh Mullen 10/1818 & burial record for Hugh Mullen in 1840 provide the material for Martha.[16]

13. John [3] **(John** [2]**, Thomas** [1]**)** b 1779, d 1831, m2 Mary Persons (Parsons), Priscilla Wood.   Abundant   records; known usually as Rev. John. Land records & [1810 & 1830]. There are two Findagrave   records   #s 6875061 & 13079974, the latter w/ a biography.

Children of John [3] & Mary Parsons Welborn[17]

21	i.	Martha	b1801 d 1879 m John Hilton
22	ii.	Jane	b 1803 d 1886 m Wm Robbins
23	iii.	William J.	b 4/1808
24	iv.	Evans	b 3/1812
25	v.	John	b 1814
26	vi.	Terry Scott	b 6/1816

---

[16] M record, County Court Records at Asheboro, NC in FHL #s 0019641, & 0019658.

Findagrave #64710632, with photo of stone.

[17] Issue of John & Mary Parsons are given in The Family bible-footnote 8.

The [1850] for Priscilla Welborn contains the following issue (all in given-name initials); J.W. James Wood; S.E. Sally Eliza; W.K. Wiley Kimball.

U.S. census
1850 Randolph Co, North, Priscilla Welborn household. roll 641, p172A, family 139.

27	vii.	Parsons	b ?1805 or 1815
28	viii.	Mary (= Polly) b 3/1818 d 1911 m John Coltrane.	

Children of John [3] & Priscilla Wood

29	viiii.	James W(ood)	b 9/1820 d 6/1864 m Elizabeth Jane McNairy
30	ix.	Nancy b 1822 d 4/1902 m John Dorsett	
31	x.	Logan b? d 1824	inferred from estate
32	xi.	Sally Eliza b 4/1827 d ? One census record.	
33	xii.	Wiley Kimball b1829 d 1899 m Miranda E. Holmes.	

14 William [3] (John [2], Thomas [1]) b 1785, d 1832, m Patsey Lacey (=Martha). William was an important figure in early 19th Century Randolph Co, leaving many records (~ 28 in The DataBase). He was a Justice of The Peace & active at court. Interestingly enough, he died intestate in 1832. Martha was enrolled in [1850] with two daughters, Elizabeth & Martha. [18]

Children of William [3] & Martha (Patsey) Welborn

34	i.	Jesse	b1812- d 1836. Estate records.
35	ii.	William Ruffin b 1823- d 1843. bible (footnote 8).	
36	iii.	Cyrus b 1824- d 2/1865. m Yevena Hinshaw.	
37	iv.	Susan (Susannah) b 1816 m David Coltrane.	

---

[18] e g 1816, administrator for estate of G. Gray. RGGJ XXXII, Martha Welborn household. Roll 641, p183,family 295(sic). Elizabeth 22, Martha 20.

1832 d intestate, wife Martha. Findagrave #46793903 w/good stone. North Carolina Estate Files, 1663-1979, Randolph Co, FamilySearch.org.

38	v.	Nancy b 1820- d 1850. m Franklin Gardner.
39	vi.	Eliz. Jane b 1827 m Franklin Gardner 1851.
40	vii.	Martha M. B 1829 m Thomas Hanner 2/1852.
41	viii.	Joseph O.P. bible only.

16 Joseph [3] (John [2], Thomas [1]) b 1790, d 1875, m Parthenia G. W. Saxton in 1826. Joseph M. (in most records) served in the State Guard 1817 through, at least, 1820; first as a Captain & later promoted to Major. The [1830] Randolph Co found him next to his brother William, Esq. And together with[1840 1850 & finally 1870], a complete parsing of their issue is possible. He is buried in the Family's Bell-Welborn cemetery next to his wife Parthenia. [19]

Children of Joseph M. [3] & Parthenia Welborn

42	i.	Mary Ann b1827 d 1922 m Thos Clark Fentress
43	ii.	Elijah(Elisha) b 1828 d 1900 m Margaret Clark
44	iii.	William L. b 1829 d 1920 m2 Parmelia & Eliz. Julian.
45	iv.	Frederick D. b 1831 d 1885 m2 Mary Tulbert, Mrs Mollie Brown.
46	v.	Martha Jane b 1833 d 1911 m Joseph or Henry Farlow.

---

[19] Vital data from Family bible, Family History Library Catalog , FHL US/CAN Film 18067, item 3, p 56 (footnote 8).

The m recorded in the bible as well as NCDAH record 01 289.   The RCGJ recorded both the State Guard items: XXXIV(1) & XXXIV(2), pps 40,43.

The Findagrave #s 62828449 & 62829637. Both stones appear to be original.

47	vi.	Eliz. Ellen Hinshaw.	b 1836 d 1906	m James
48	vii.	Sarah J. Swaim.	b 1838 d >1920	m Chas.
49	viii.	Linden McGee b 1839 d 1863		CSA 1st NC
50	ix.	David L.	b 1843 d ?	No information
51	x.	Robert Mc (sic) b 1847 d 1925 m Minera Dicks.		

19 Jesse³ (John ²,Thomas ¹) b 1795, d 1875 m Edith Simmons. A tax document dated 1813 suggests Jesse was ~ 18 & a land owner. Substituting for the missing [1820] in Randolph Co, is a tax record for 1 wp & 1 blk on Muddy Creek. Jesse served as a Captain in the militia as well as in the office of Coroner. While the [1850] is missing, he was enrolled in [1830, 1840, & 1860– at age 65]. As were most of his Family, burial was in the Bell-Welborn cemetery.[20]

---

[20] The marriage appears in The Family bible (as Edith), footnote 8, & in an NCSA index of marriages, p 96 (as Edy).

The tax records: 1813 RCGJ IX(2), p5ff: 1820: Grigg, Barbara N. & Carolyn N. Hager, 1820 Tax List, Randolph County North Carolina. Randolph County Historical Society, Asheboro, 1978, p17.

1822 as Captain in the militia– General Court Martial, RCGJ XXXIV(2), p46 (along with Joseph. They were both acquitted.)

U. S. Census, Randolph Co, NC

1830, Jesse Wilborn household. Roll 125, p 31, line 24. The age distribution presents a puzzle: 2 60-70, 40-50 (which must be Jesse) w/no females. Near William, Esq. & Joseph.

1840, Jesse Welborn household. Roll 369, page 89, line 3. Again an age distribution puzzle: 40-50 (Jesse) w/ a 10-15 male & a 20-30 couple.

1860, Jesse Wilborn household. Roll 910, page 144, w/Edith age 60, bNC.

Findagrave #62827612 w/ good stone.

Children of Jesse [3] & Edith Welborn
As the marriage was in 1854 & the census presents many questions, following any issue will require additional work.

FAMILY B   JAMES WELBORN Progenitor

Précis

    This is a large Family. James & Mary Isabella Teague have been credited with nine sons & at least four daughters. The succeeding two generations were accordingly populated: a total of 60+ descendants in three Generations are treated here.

    James Welborn (of various early spellings) was born in Maryland in 1737 came to the Granville District of North Carolina & with Mary settled in the Abbotts Creek region of,n, Rowan County- today's Davidson County.[1] The earliest records for James were land records in 1759 & 1762, both in Abbotts Creek & near the family of Moses Teague. The pair together with most of the Family moved to Barren Co KY about 1805; James leaving a will there in 1811. The will specifies wife Esabel [sic], sons Samuel, Joshua (as executor)

---

[1]   James parents were William, b 1/1713 in MD, married Ann Crabtree, date; and died ??. Barnes, Robert W., Baltimore County Families 1659-1759, GPC 1989, pps 690, 702. Also from Baldwin (Cotton), Jane, Maryland Calendar of Wills, v VI, 1726-1730. Family Line Publications, Westminster, 1988.

    Two self-published books need mentioning here: Wilburn, Hiram C., Welborn-Wilburn History, Genealogy. Micro-reproduction of the original published Waynesville N.C. Miller Printing, Asheville, 1953. Available FHL film 1421486. This early volume is now thoroughly discredited as the proper MD references are missing & Hiram attributes James to [a] Samuel Welborn & his wife Mary Chapley all of Accomack County VA. Some of the FamilyTree records, however, point to this reference.

Welborn, Gene, Welborns and related families with roots in North and South Carolina. By author, Greenwood SC,1994. This book contains the proper MD material & useful information on a number of families including more modern generations. However, it is poorly documented in the early decades.

with Gideon a witness. No daughters are named. [2]

The burial of James & Mary Isabella Teague is given in the Poplar Log Church Cemetery in Barren County, Kentucky. [3]

Owing primarily to the size of the Family, there are a number of puzzles revealed by what information is available that must be solved if a reliable Formal Genealogy is to be built.

The number of children of James & Mary Isabella.

Eight sons are listed in his will and/or in various land records. A ninth son, John, designated as such in a Family bible record is not included in the will or land records, although his d o b is known– 1786. [4]

---

[2] James was a chain carrier for Moses Teague & John Fullerlane, 1759. Hofmann, Margaret, Granville District NC 1848-1763 v 3, by author 1989 Ahoskia NC. #s 4672 121-G & 4917 129-G.

His Will abstract is in Peden, E. C., comp., Barren County Kentucky Will Book No. 1. by author., Glasgow KY, 1979, p 33. (There are also complete transcripts available on Ancestry.com's Public Member Trees.)

[3] Findagrave *#23367795 & 42088618*. No stones are shown: his dates as 1736-1811 and hers as 1742-1821. The marriage data given by Ancestry.com from the U.S. & International Marriage Records claims VA, KY, & NC as the location– the former probably correct. A Family Data Collection gives her parents as Moses Teague, Sr & Elizabeth Loftin & states 1742 as her d o b. West, Edmund, The Family Data Collection- Births. On-line database, Ancestry.com Operations, accessed 2001.

[4] Findagrave #77333504.

Linn, Jo White, Abstracts of the Court of Common Pleas and Quarter Sessions, vol 2, pub by author, 1977, p125. A deed transfer from Wm Spurgin to Moses, Aaron, Will [sic], James, Isaac, Gidion, & Samuel Welborn all sons of Jas Wilborn Sr: 8 July 1771, Book 3, folio 286..Sons Joshua & John had not yet been born.

In order to investigate the ninth son John, it is necessary to establish as close as possible the birth order and dates-of-birth of the eight sons. This is accomplished here by means of census, court, & the 1768 tax & 1792 petition of Rowan County. The d o b from the non-census information is based on the 18th century age requirements for holding property (16) & for majority (18 or 21); for /s/ petitions assumed here to be 18. Accordingly, the Welborn signers in 1768 must have been born before 1750 & for 1792, 1774.[5]

The marriage date of James and Mary Isabella is not known, but various FamilyTree sources claim 1756. As it is fairly firm that her d o b was 1742, these specify her age at the m as 14!

The birth dates given, again, by a FamilyTree source are: Aaron b 10/1760; William b 9/1761 ; James Jr b 8/1764; Isaac b 1765 Gideon b 1767; Samuel b 1770; Joshua b 9/1780; Moses b 7/1783 & John b 9/1786. Here, the oldest, Aaron, was b with Mary Isabella age 18 .[6]

Note that only two are established from direct reference– William's 1761 from the Family bible; John's from his burial record.. If the dates above are correct, Mary Isabella gave birth to her youngest, John, at age 44.

In the present work, the dates above agree with the independent estimates based upon other than census data mentioned; with the important exception of the date of 1783 for Moses. As argued below & in the Formal Genealogy, this Moses was actually the

------

[5]   The 1768 tax list is in the NCGSJ IX(4), pp 39-46. The two /s/ were James B1& Isaac whose identity is discussed in Chapter Four.

The 1792 petition (for a new county) appeared in the Rowan County Register 13(1), p2908. /s/ were James, Isaac, Samuel, John, & Gideon.

[6]   No evidence is supplied by this source for the month & year dates– it gives however a correct translation of James' Will.
Information on the vital data for the sons available on FamilyTree ranges widely.

son of Moses B2, b c1758 d 1783.

In addition, the FamilyTree & DAR information includes four daughters of James & Mary I., with d o b ranging from 1769 to1774.[7]

Parsing the census for James provides excellent evidence that the 1786 John is included in the Family of James & Mary I., and some evidence of the daughters. In [1790] the 2/3/4 distribution is resolved as James Sr & William 'B0' (see Chapter Four) both b<1775; Samuel b c1770; Joshua b 1774; & John b1786 (the three youngest). The four females include M. Isabella, and three; Elizabeth A. b 1769; Ruth b 1764; Anna b 1776; & Caroline b 1776 (twins). In [1800 & 1810] both John & Joshua appear in the correct age groups

Following the histories of the B2 sons of James, we find west- & southward migration to Pendleton Co SC, Barren Co KY, & St Francois Co MO. Two of the sons remained in NC (William and John). James jr originally went to SC along with Aaron, but later moved westward to St. Francois County MO. Accordingly, a number of Generation 3 of Family B left records there. A history of the County published in about 1899, giving mainly biographical accounts; and an abstract of wills enables determination of the following:[8]

Isaac B2 moved from KY to St. Francois Co MO in c1821. He died there intestate in 1824. His history involving the journey from NC to MO is complicated: an [1810] in Barren Co KY with his

[7] Texas DAR, The Roster of Texas Daughters Revolutionary Ancestors, Texas, 1967, p2249.

[8] Saint Francois County, Missouri History and Biographies, pub by Mountain Press, Signal Mountain TN, 2006. p81. This reference is a copy of a work published in about 1889 (from the dates included in the text) that Mountain Press does not explicitly acknowledge– while providing information one wishes for better documentation.

father & brothers suggests he stopped on the way west. At this point, some conjecture is called for: the [1820] Cumberland Co KY lists Samuel with an extensive Family (eight males) with two in age class b <1776. This strongly suggests a brother (their father d 1811) complete with Family. In Monroe Co , same census, we find a Peggy Welborn b c1775 with a group that includes Joshua & William.[9] As these are all surely Family B, Peggy needs to be identified. She appears in all census [1820 to 1840] always next to, or near, a Family B son– she must be so associated. (As she had issue, we assume she was a wife of a Family B, probably Generation 2).

A hypothesis that is consistent with all of the above: Isaac on his way west from NC stops off in KY with the Family, staying from roughly 1805 to 1821/2. He stays with brother Samuel in 1820 before leaving for MO. In so doing, he leaves his wife (Margaret=Peggy) & family behind– either abandoning them or intending to send for them later.
However he dies intestate! before doing so. This tale has

---

[9]   U.S. census
1810 Barren Co KY, Isaac Wilbourn household, Roll 5, p45 (the index lists him twice). Age class 1765-1784.
1820 Cumberland Co KY, Samuel Wilbourn household, Roll 19, p 159, 4th from bottom. Two males >45, b <1776; one male each younger age classes- presumably of Samuel.
1820 Monroe Co KY, Peggy Welborn household, Roll 25, p 115;line 18 (Family group lines 16,19)
1830 Monroe Co KY, Peggy Welborn household, Roll 39, p 399, line 12.
1840 Monroe Co KY, Margaret Welborn household, Roll 120, p 253, line 10. Age class 60-70. The [1810 & 1820] combined give an age range for Isaac of 1765-1776. Thus, the two are of the same age.
   Brief Co history: Barren & Cumberland both created 1799; Monroe from both in 1820. The land holdings of the Family are not specific, and it is quite possible that their holdings were in all three- or e g the Monroe Co being the same as one of the two previous.

the advantage that it can account for Peggy and the combined [1820] with both him & brother Samuel enrolled.

The biography (previous footnote) credits him with a son, Isaac jr, b 1806 who married Jemima Matkin about 1830. This B3 couple produced six children, of whom in 1888 only two were still living: Samuel P. b 1841 married Elizabeth Sanders, [1830] St Francois MO; Thomas, Samuel, & Isaac all age group 1800-1810 w/James (Jr) 1760-1770; and William F. (From a parse, one son b 1800-1810 is missing.)

The problem of the multiple Moseses.

There is a major problem with the name Moses. One of James & Mary I.'s sons was a Moses who was not named in the Will nor in the Family bible (below). In Generation 3, the record points to three Moseses, perhaps all in Family B, but with parentage to be determined.

Generation 2

Moses, son of James the Progenitor of Family B, was b c1758 and d in 1783, living only some 25 years. The order given in the 1771 deed transfer (footnote 4) is perhaps in birth order, but does not indicate if all had reached majority status. If Moses had, his d o b would be 1755. His 1783 estate record is from Surry County– the estate was transferred to Rowan County by his mother Mary Isabella neé Teague as Administrator. (His wife Martha née Teague was a buyer). The author of Surry County Wills, Mrs. J.W. Linn explains that the "moveable estate" applies to all inventory other than land. Why this Moses had presence in Surry County is not clear– there are no records found there.[10]

---

[10]   Book 2:6. Inventory of moveable estate of Moses Wilborn dcd returned by Mary Welborn, administrator. Received Feb Court 1783. Book 2:11 Inventory of the Estate of Moses Welborn, returned

In 1778 and/or 1780 this Moses was taxed in Rowan Co. Census [1810] shows two in Rowan Co, one in age class 1765-1784; the other 1785-1794: B2 & tentatively B3.[11] Additional reliable records available for Moses, and his son (?) Moses (see below), are military ones. In the War of 1812 records, a Captain Moses Welborn served in the 4th NC Regiment. An explicit Moses Jr Welborn was a Lt. in the same Regiment.[12]

Next, tax records are extant for 1815 Rowan Co both Moses Sr & Jr Wilbourne were included, Moses Sr taxed on 217A & Jr with 265A.[13] Although these may seem to point to a father-son duo, we must withhold such a conclusion– at least until Generation 3 is treated.

Generation 3

Together with the military & tax records, [1810] and [1820], two Moses were enrolled in Rowan Co NC. In the same two census, a single Moses appears in the Pendleton Co SC schedule, providing

---

by John Teague. Buyers included James & Martha. Linn, Jo White, Surry County, North Carolina Wills 1771-1827. Genealogical Publishing Co, Baltimore, 1992. pps 45, 47.

[11] NCSA C.R. 085.701.5 p30, #18 &/or Ancestry.com facsimile source: List of Taxable Property in the County of Rowan NC 1778, indexed by Annie W. Burns, p11.
U.S. census Rowan Co NC
1810 Moses Wilborne household, Roll 43, p 260, line 7; age class 1765-1784.
1810 Moses Wilbourne household, Roll 43, pages 257/8; age class 1785-1794.

[12] Muster Rolls of the Soldiers of the War of 1812: detached from The Militia of North Carolina, in 1812 and 1814. Pub by the General Assembly January 21, 1851. Reprinted GPC 1980, p123.

[13] Linn, Jo W. , Rowan County Tax List 1815, Salisbury NC, privately pub., 1987, p30.

the evidence for three Generation 3 Moses.[14]

#1 The Moses of Rowan (& Davidson) Counties b Nov 5, 1782, - d Aug 7, 1820. Burial was in Abbotts Creek Primitive Baptist Church Cemetery, Davidson Co. There are two Findagraves that agree on the burial location & d o b , but disagree on the date of death Aug 7, 1820 or 1826. One gives the parents as General William Wellborn & Prudence Davis Wellborn, and his wife née Elizabeth Mock. Census [1820] in Rowan.

The Family bible entry does include the following: "Major William Welborn of Guilford Co, b. 9-26-1761, d. 12-26-1841; son of James Welborn and wife Isabella ---- , mar. 1st Prudence Davis and had *at least* four children: ....." (Author's italics). In addition, no mention of Moses, or any of the children of William & Prudence, are in his 1841 will. However the Lafayette Co MO 1877 Atlas gives a brief bio of Jacob Welborn, son of Moses & Prudence. The entry also gives the correct grandparents.[15]

In addition, an 1826 Probate record for this Moses exists that includes the names William, Samuel, the widow and Family. The names William & Samuel are both of Family B and Rowan County– presumably Generation 3.[16] The 1792 Rowan Co petition contains no

---

[14] With footnotes 12, 13.
U. S. Census, Pendleton Co SC
1810 Moses Wilborn household, Roll 61, p 252, line 21. Next to James b<1766.
1820 Moses Wilbourne household, Roll 120, p 206, line 17.

[15] Ancestry.com, Lafayette County, Missouri, Excerpts from the 1877 Atlas (Original Matthews, A.H. Missouri Publishing Co., 1877). This Ancestry citation is just that– it is not searchable. The entry here is contributed, but is available under a search for Jacob Welborn.

[16]   U. S. Census
1820 Rowan Co NC, Moses Wilburn househ0old. Roll 81, p318, line 40. Age class 1776-1794.
Findagrave # 15435841; also #89269176. Wallburg Cemetery

/s/ named Moses: his d o b specifies that he was 10. (footnote 5) It does contain, however, the names of James B1 as well as most of his sons.

Moses #1 is clearly identified.

#2 The Posey County, IN Moses.

There is a Findagrave record for a Moses Welborn b Jul 4, 1784- d Jun 11, 1851. The photo of a stone, somewhat modern- looking, obscures the vital data. The burial site is the Timothy Downen Cemetery in Blairsville, Posey Co, IN. The parents are incorrectly given as James b1736 d 1811 B1! & Isabella Teague Welborn.[17] This Moses has [1840 & 1850] for Posey Co IN that gives his age as 67, b 1783 in NC & a wife Deborah b 1788 in NC. The [1830] for Guilford County does include a Moses with the correct age class.[18] The biographical information in the Histories of Posey & Gibson Counties supports this census as of the Posey Co Moses.

Davidson Co.
Family History Library Catalog , FHL US/CAN Film 18067, item 3, p173.
North Carolina Estate Files, 1663-1979; FamilySearch.org "index & images" images 3,10, & 14 of 14.

[17] Findagrave # 69414025. This skip of a Generation seems pervasive in much of the FamilyTree information.

[18]   U.S. census
1830 Guilford Co NC, Moses Willborn household. Roll 121, p 202, line 7. Moses is in age class 40-50. (Mention needs made here of a what appears to be a census duplication. Mons (sic) is also listed on p 168 with, however, a different male age class makeup (the female distribution is the same). The handwriting on both is difficult. This problem is treated in Chapter Four.)
U. S. Census Posey Co IN
1840 Moses Welborn household, Roll 90, p 325, line 9.
1850 Moses Welborn household, Roll 166, p319, family 973. Wife Deborah 62NC.

> The family was founded in Indiana by Moses
> Welborn, a native of North Carolina, who was
> born in Guilford county, near Guilford court
> house July 4, 1783. He came to Posey County in
> 1833 and located at Mt. Vernon, subsequently
> entering land at the forks of Big Creek, which
> he developed into productive farm land. He
> died in 1851, a victim of the cholera scourge
> of that year. He married, about 1808, Deborah
> Chipman, born on November 3, 1787.[19]

As no census for Moses B2 exists (he d 1783) we must use evidence available to place this Moses' parents. The key seems to be the duplication of Moses, Sr & Jr in the 1812 military & 1815 tax records (footnotes 12,13). In addition, Moses #1 was deceased in 1840, & #3 (below) was in SC.

Thus, we conclude that Moses #2 was the son of Moses B2.

#3 The South Carolina Moses

In SC, a Moses Welborn appears in census (footnote 14), the Findagrave archive, and in a single military record.[20]

Burial: b Mar. 14, 1786 - d Aug 25, 1834. The photo is of a very modern-looking stone that clearly does not date to 1834. An

---

[19] The text is a biographical sketch of Francis M. son of Samuel P. who in turn was of Moses Welborn of Guilford Co NC. Leffel, John C., ed. History of Posey County (IN), Standard Pub. Co, Chicago, 1913. p 319. Also mentioned in History of Gibson County Co IN available on-line Ancestry.com, images 785,6 of the book.

[20] Findagrave # 9697062. Again the included family link cannot be relied on.

Moss, Bobby G., Roster of South Carolina Patriots in the American Revolution. Genealogical Publishing Co., Baltimore, 1983.

inscription on it credits him with service in the SC militia in the war of 1812. The burial is in the Big Creek Cemetery, Williamston, Anderson Co SC. The 1812 military record lists him as a Corporal in Nash's Regiment, South Carolina Volunteers. (U.S. War of 1812 Service Records,1812-1815, Ancestry.com on-line database). In [1810 & 1820] he is enrolled in Pendleton County. In the former he is in age class 1784-1794 & occurs next to James Wilborn b<1766. In the latter he is in class 1775-1794, one family from Thomas Wilbourne, age class <1776.

This SC Moses presents a problem as his 'neighbors' in Pendleton Co all belong to Family A, this Chapter. In the Family bible reference for this Family no Moses appears. However, in [1810] this Moses is listed next to a James b<1766 & who is almost certainly a Generation 2. A reasonable candidate is James (junior) B2. The nearby Thomas, in [1820] is identified as Generation 2 of Family A.[21]

The number and identity of children of Samuel & Joshua

These are two of the younger (B2) sons of James who moved to KY along with most of the Family. The establishment of their issue is problematic owing to the lack of wills; the proximity of the Families; and some missing & confusing census. We resort to parsing the existing census– a risky business, but which may provide some clues.

Samuel had [1800] in Rowan Co; [1810] in Barren Co KY; [1820] in Cumberland Co KY; & [1830] in Russell Co KY.[22] In the

---

[21]   U. S. Census Pendleton Co SC

1810 Moses Wilborne household. Roll 61, p 252, line 21 (next to James b<1766).

1820 Moses Wilbourne household. Roll 120, p 206, line 17.

1830 Anderson Co (Pendleton) Moses Williams (sic) household. Roll 173, p 151, line 4.

[22]   U. S. Census

1800 Rowan Co NC, Samuel Wilburn household. Roll 33, p 370, line 9.

first, the only young male enrolled was Samuel Jr b 1790 whose subsequent history was in Guilford Co & with 2 females <10 & a wife the age of Samuel Sr

By [1820] he had acquired sons 1800-1810 & 1794-1800 & four females 1794-1810– his wife, again, the same age. The [1820], mentioned above in the Isaac B2 story, is a hybrid Family– aside from identifying the two eldest as Samuel & Isaac, the identity of Isaac's children enrolled is not known.

But in [1830], Samuel in Russell Co (Monroe) is listed next to James b 1800-10 & Jesse b 1790- 1800. These two fit the [1820] parse exactly. (James remained in Russell Co & was enrolled in [1850]). However, there are two 1800-1810; a 1810-1815; & a 1820-1825 males that are unaccounted for. The four females, again, remain unknown. [23]

The parsing of B2 Joshua allows a very few children to be identified. In [1800] Rowan Co, a male b 1790-1800 can be Joshua Jr. The [1810] in Barren KY showed 3 sons b 1800-1810; these identified as William b 1799, Joshua Jr b c1804, & Jacob b 1809. Two young daughters, 1800-1810, are indicated with no further information. By [1820] Joshua now in Monroe Co KY had, again, three young sons b 1810-1820 (Jacob was one); & two b 1794-1804. Six daughters b 1810-1820, 1804-1810, & 1794-1804.

For both [1830 & 1840] in Monroe Co, missing issue is

1810 Barren Co KY, Samuel Wilbourn household. Roll 5, p 46, family group lines 16-19.
1820 Cumberland Co KY, Samuel Wilbourn household. Roll 19, p 159, 4th from bottom.
1830 Russell Co KY, Samuel Wilbourn household. Roll 41, p 122, lines 5th from bottom.
See also footnote 9 for Co sequence.

[23] FamilyTree & Findagrave specify a first wife, Rachel, b 1770 d 1790. Samuel Jr thus could have been of Rachel. The name of his second wife is not known, but see Chapter Four..

there– at least 3 sons b 1820-1830 & 5 daughters. And a John of Monroe Co KY & Monroe Co IN, [1840,50,60] respectively: the indicated d o b is consistent at 1798 & fits Joshua in [1800] & [1820], but not in [1810]. In [1840] he is listed next to Joshua. This individual is included in Chapter Four. [24]

In summary, there are many unidentified W-s associated with Joshua in the KY region thru 1870, and attempting to place them will require documentation & future study.

We acknowledge the hazards of frontier life in these times. In Joshua's case the large numbers of missing taken as indicating deaths would seem excessive. This result is a definite hindrance in establishing a Generation 3, Family B.

FORMAL GENEALOGY

Generation 1
1. James Welborn[1] vital data b1737, d 1811; m Mary Isabella Teague b 1742 d 1821. Will dated 1811 in Barren Co, KY. His first Rowan Co record was a 1759 land survey; land acquisition, 634A along Abbotts Creek, followed by two more in the same locale

---

[24] U. S. Census
1800 Rowan Co NC, Joshua Wilburn household. Roll 33, p 371, line 1. One male <10 is ?Joshua Jr.
1810 Barren Co KY, Joshua Wilbourn household. Roll 5, p 46, the Family group.
1820 Monroe Co KY, Joshua Welborn household. Roll 25, p 205, again Family group, lines 16-18.
1830 Monroe Co KY, Joshua Wilborn household. Roll 390, p 399,line 10. Peggy, line 11.
1840 Monroe Co KY, Joshua Willborn household. Roll 120, p 253, lines 8-10.
1850 Monroe Co KY, Joshua Wilborn household. Roll 213, p 429A, family 900. Joshua age 70, Rachel (nee Smith?)67, Jacob 40, Margaret (Peggy) 30.
There are three census for William the most important [1850] giving his d o b & his wife Elizabeth b VA.

in 1762 (700A) & 1764.[25] In 1771 a deed abstract listed James Sr and his sons (footnote 6). Owning land in both Rowan & Randolph Cos., he sold 200A along Bush Creek to his brother William (Family C) in 1794. Among his other records (there are over 40 in the DataBase) are a 1768 tax; the /s/ of the 1792 petition; and the [1790 & 1800].[26] The move to Barren Co, KY occurred after the [1800] as his first and only census there was [1810]. The heirs were Esabel [sic]; sons Samuel & Joshua with Gideon the executor. Burial was in the Poplar Log cemetery, Barren Co[27]

---

[25] Hofmann, Margaret M., The Granville District of North Carolina, 1748-1763, Abstracts of Grants, vol 3(Rowan). by author, Waldon NC , The Roanoke News, 1987.

      & MARS 12.13.131.16 & 12.12.81.43, a very large land owner.

[26] The 1792 Rowan Co petition is in The Rowan County Register v13(#1), p2908.

      Linn, Jo White, Lists of Taxables in Rowan County, 1768, Abstract of the Minutes of the Court of Pleas & Quarter Sessions, 1774, v II, p198.

      James of Rowan Co grantor to Isaac York, 200A Bush Creek originally granted to Wm Welborn, Nov 1790. John Welborn proved. Deed Book 8: 172: RCGJ XXIX(3). Reference illustrates the close relationship of the two. In 1805 James in preparation of the move to KY sold more of the Bush Creek property to Enoch Davis: RCGJ XXIX(3), p36.

[27] U. S. Census
1790 Salisbury District (Rowan), Roll 7, p 322.
1800 Rowan Co, James Wilburn household, Roll 33, p370.
1810 Barren Co KY, James Wilbourn household, Roll 5, p46, line 17.

      WillBook 1; p159:King, J.E.S., Early Kentucky Wills. Reprint GPC 1969 (1933), p6.

      Findagrave #42088618- added material gives his parents as William b1712 & Ann Crabtree b1714- see footnote 3.

The children of James [1] & Mary Isabella:

+	2.	i.	Isaac	b c1765.
+	3	ii.	Moses	b c1758
+	4	iii.	Aaron	b1760.
+	5	iv.	William	b 1761.
+	6	v.	James (Jr)	b 1764.
+	7	vi.	Gideon	b 1767.
+	8	vii.	Samuel	b c1770.
+	9	viii.	Joshua	b c1780.
+	10	ix.	John	b 1786.
	11	x.	Elizabeth A.	b 1769 m John Swift, James W-., bond.
	12	xi.	Ruth	b1764 m Robert Parsons
	13	xii.	Anna	b 1776
	14	xiii.	Caroline	b 1776 [28]

Generation 2

2. Isaac Welborn [2] (James [1]) b c1765, d 1824; m ?Margaret ? In [1790] he apparently was married, (1/1/1). He /s/ the 1792 Rowan Co petition along with members of the Family. There are eight land records in the DataBase, indicating him as an active land owner.[29]

About 1805 he went west to Barren Co KY, along with most of the Family, & appeared in the [1810] there, but not in [1820 or 1830].

---

[28] The daughters are from the Texas Society of the DAR, The Roster of Texas Daughters of Revolutionary Ancestors, vol. 4, 1976.

[29] e. g. 1787 MARS 12.14.107.2798: state grant 1789, 200A Grasy Branch (sic). And " Isaac Wilborn Jr late of Rowan Co to Joshua.... land conveyed to grantee by his father James Wilborn.... " 3 Dec 1794. Establishes in one the father & two of his sons, and the fact that Isaac had left Rowan Co . Kluttz, James, Abstracts of Rowan Co Deed Books, Deed Book 14, item 2564, p 9. Many of Family B's land records are in the Kluttz series.

Moreover, he is not mentioned in James' will. The details of his history there is told above– he died intestate in 1824 in St Francois Co MO.[30]

Children of Isaac [2] & ?Margaret

+   15   i.   Isaac Jr   b 1806
          ii.   *John*   *b c1800   parse only*

3. Moses Welborn [2] (James [1]) b c1758, d 1783; m Martha Teague b 1762 d 1815. In 1771, like all his brothers, he appeared in a deed transfer to James. (Footnote 4). His d o b is estimated assuming him to be about Martha's age. In 1783 the Estate was moved from Surry to Rowan Co by Grandmother Mary Isabella giving an estimate of the date of d: accordingly, he lived but about 25 years. His only appearance during that span are (were) two tax records The m of Moses & Martha Teague is proved by burial record [31]

---

[30]   U.S. census
1790 Salisbury Dist. NC (Rowan), Isaac {Jr} Wilborn household, Roll 7, p322.
1810 Barren Co KY, Isaac Wilbourn household, Roll 5, p 45, w/Family group lines 16-19.
The 1792 petition: Linn, Jo White, The Rowan County Register, v 13(1), Feb 1998, p 2908.
The biography- St Francois Co Records, Mountain Press, p22.
The parse of John comes from the [1840] Monroe KY, listed next to Margaret, footnote 9.

[31] Linn, Jo White, Surry County, North Carolina Wills 1771-1827. Genealogical Publishing Co, Baltimore, 1992. (Book 2, folio 11), p47.
        1778 w/father James in Capt. Davis' District,- Linn, Jo White, Abstracts of Wills & Estate Records of Rowan County, 1753-1805 and Tax Lists 1759 & 1778. By author, Salisbury, 1980. pz.
        1780 tax in NCSA C. R. 085.701.5, p30,#18.
        Findagrave #7731041 w/ a very good stone photo.

The children of Moses [2] & Martha Welborn

+   16   i.   Moses (Jr)   b 1806

4. Aaron Welborn [2] (James [1]) b c1760, d ?1843: m Elizabeth Younger in 1782. All vital data is estimated or in undocumented information.[32] Rowan Co recorded a tax in 1783– the only apparent record before he moved to Pendleton Co, SC. A brief summary of Aaron's life in that Co (along with his brother James) is given by Wooley. Successive census (1790 thru 1830) provide good material for parsing his issue & allowing an estimate of his d o b.[33]

The Children of Aaron [2] & Elizabeth Welborn[34]

---

[32] FamilyTree contributed. There is a Findagrave, but a useless one as there is no stone- just the d o b & d date & the admission that burial is unknown #40912696.

[33] The summary, Wooley, James E., Ed., A Collection of Upper South Carolina Genealogical and Family Reords, v 1, Southern Historical Press, Easley SC, 1979, p335. Includes his m to Eliz. Younger.
          U. S. Census
1790 Pendleton Co SC, Aaron Welborn household, First Census of the United States, Ninety-Six District, p82 (distribution 1/2/3)
1800 Pendleton Co SC, Aaron Wilburn household, Roll 50, p 160, family 838.
1810 Pendleton Co SC, Aaron Wilbourn household, Roll 61, p158A, line 8 (next to Elisha).
1820 missing.
1830 Anderson Co SC, Aaron Wilbourn household, Roll 173, p 147, 4th from bottom.

[34] parse: unaccounted, male[1800] 4<10 , continued [1810] 3 <10 & [1820] 1804-1810 / females [1800] 1 10-16. An Elisha b1784 to AR fits, but not included.

+	17	i.	Anna	b 1780	m Duckworth
+	18	ii.	James	b c1784	
+	19	iii.	Thomas	b 1790	
+	20	iv.	Ruth	b 1793	m Duckworth
+	21	v.	Aaron (Jr)	b 1794	
+	*22*	*vi.*	*Elisha*	*b 1797/9*	
+	23	vi.	Gideon	b 1801	
+	24	vii.	Younger	b 1805	

5. William Welborn [2] (James [1]) b 1761, d 1842, m2 Prudence Davis 1787; Rachel Payne 1770-179? in 1807. His history is in a Family bible, although not complete as all of Prudence's children are, as noted, not entered. Will Book 6, folio 116 in Guilford Co contains his will, with Rachel & the youngest children as heirs.[35]   The 1792 Rowan Co petition (for a new County) was signed by the six brothers ; William, Gideon, John, Samuel, Isaac, & James (Jr)– Footnote 4. In The War of 1812 William was a member of the 4th Regiment of 4th Company with records in 1813 & 1814– although in the latter he was listed as a deserter.[36]   There are numerous land records dating from 1791 thru 1826, and census from [1790] thru [1820]. Burial was in Davidson Co in 1841.[37]

---

[35] Family History Library Catalog , FHL US/CAN Film 18067, item 3.

   The Will in Guilford Co, Book C, #116. Author has copy.

[36] RCGJ VIII(2), p28 & Records of the Adjutant General of Militia, NCGJ 37(4), p 367.

[37] e.g. 1791 Abshire Ms. W.O., Stokes Co Deeds I(ii), p 217 (he apparently had land in both Rowan & Stokes Cos.) Shoaf, Mary Jo Davis, Davidson County North Carolina Abstracts of Wills, Book 2, 1844-1868, & Deed Book 3 1826-1828. Pub by author, Roanoke VA, 1989.

   U. S. Census, Rowan Co NC

Children of William [2] & Prudence[38]

+	25	i.	Samuel	b 1790
+	26	ii.	Cary	b 1792
+	27	iii.	Davis	b 1792
+	<u>28</u>	iv.	*Moses*	b 1784 d1851 as above in text

Children of William[2] & Rachel

+	29	iv.	Thomas	b 1808
+	30	v.	Barnabas	b 1812
+	31	vi.	Wisdom	b 1816
	32	vii.	Elizabeth	b 1820 In Will, m Welch
+	33	viii.	Isaac P.	b 1822

6. James Jr. Welborn [2] (James [1])   b 1764, d 1841, m Rebecca Younger (footnote 32 w/Aaron) As with all sons of James Sr, except Joshua & John, he is listed in the deed transfer of 1771 (footnote 4) and in the brief biography with Aaron.[39] There are no Rowan Co records to be found, and he removed to SC early on,

---

1790 William Wilborn household, Roll 7, p322 In the same census there is William Sr with distribution 1/3/2. This Wm is identified as Generation 0– see Chapter Four.
1800 William Wilburn household, Roll 33, p370,line 12. (Samuel, Samuel jr & James lines 9-12.
1810 William Wilborne household, Roll 43, p 260, line14.
1820 William Willburn household, Roll 81, p 306, line 2nd bottom.
      Findagrave #17625909, Spring Hill United Methodist Cemetery, Davidson Co. No photo of stone. Rachel's burial #7732062 was in the Wallburg Cemetery, Davidson. There is a photo of the original stone, b 1770 d Feb 179? (The date not fully readable)

[38] parse [1800] two sons b 1790-1800, by Prudence,as noted in Family bible: parse uncertain owing to possibility that Rachel brought issue to m as [1810] suggests.

[39] Linn, Jo White, Rowan County Deed Abstracts, vol 1 1762-1772; Pub. by author, typescript, no date, #133. (Available Clayton Library, Houston TX; this author has page copy.)

proved by [1790] in Pendleton Co. A year later he was appointed road overseer. In [1800 & 1810] he was still in Pendleton Co, but then went west and [1830 & 1840] was in St Francois Co MO.[40] There is a contributed biography and in 1841 his will was probated. An abstract gives his heirs as his children & listed (a daughter Susanna included, but with no subsequent record). Rebecca apparently d < 1820 & may not have gone to MO.[41]

The children of James [2] Jr & Rebecca [42]

+	34	i.	Moses	b1786
+	35	ii.	Aaron	b 1794
+	36	iii.	Thomas	b 1803
+	37	iv.	James	b 1804
+	38	v.	William	b c1797
+	39	vi.	Chapley	b 1808
+	40	vii.	Carter T.	b 1811

7. Gideon Welborn [2] (James [1]) b 1767, d 1818, m Tabitha

---

[40] Appointed road overseer, 179. SCMAR index v 6 p 149.

U.S. census, Pendleton Co SC

1790 James Welborn household, Roll 21, p 8, next to Aaron.
1800 James Wilburn household, Roll 50, p 159, family 827.
1810 James Wilbourn household, Roll 61, p 262, line 20.

U. S. Census, St Francois Co MO

1830 James Welborn household, Roll 72, p 420, line 24.
1840 Carter S. Welborn household, Roll 63, p 230, line 9. W/ sons.

[41] An Ancestry.com Public Member Tree contribution carries a brief biography that agrees with his records in the present work. Mentioned, in particular, is that his place of burial is unknown.

The Will abstract is in Saint Francois County, Missouri Records, pub by Mountain Press, Signal Mountain TN, 2006. p22.

[42] Parse- generally excellent- one son 1790-1800 & one dau 1790-1800 [1800] presumably Susanna.

Stovall 1770-1830. This son of James first record (aside from the
1771 list of sons– footnote 4) is the [1790]. A year later he was
appointed tax collector– & with brothers /s/ the 1792 petition.[43]
After moving to Barren Co KY with his father, he acquired 100A of
land & in 1806 & was enrolled in [1810].[44] He was a witness to
James' Will in 1811 (Footnote 2). A Findagrave record for Gideon
gives his wife as Tabitha Stovall. There is, however, some
additional material here as Tabitha appeared in [1820] Barren Co KY,
after Gideon's d in 1818. She then acquired land in Jackson Co AL.
There is an uncertain Findagrave in AL with no stone. [45]
         Children of Gideon [2] & Tabitha[46]

----

[43] U.S. census, 1790, Salisbury District, Gidion Wilborn
household. Roll 7, p 322.
        1791 Rowan Co NC court appointed tax collector. Rowan
County Register vol 3(3), p 1095.
        1792 Rowan Co petition /s/ Gideon, John, Samuel (2),
Wm, Isaac, James. Ibid, vol 13(1), p 2908.

[44] Jillson, Willard R., The KY land Grants v 1, Chapt iv, p
439. Available Ancestry.com Operations.
        U. S. Census 1810, Barren Co KY, Gideon Wilbourn
household. Roll 5, p 43, w/Family group.

[45] For Gideon, Findagrave #97537856; there is no stone
shown. His wife given as Tabitha Stovall Welborn 1770-1830.
        U. S. Census 1820 Barren Co KY, Tabitha Wilbourn
household. Roll 17, p 30, line 2. w/ 3 sons & 3 daughters.
        Tabitha acquired land in Jackson Co AL: BLM Alabama,
Homestead and Cash Entry Patents, Pre-1908. Database on-line,
Ancestry.com Operations Inc. 1997. The issue date for 159A is 10 May
1831. Note the date discrepancy- it is possible the 1831 date was after
her death or the Findagrave date is incorrect.

[46] parse [1800] missing; [1810] 2 sons 1800-1810, 1 son
1784-1794 / 3 daus 1794-1800: these continue [1820]. William b 1805
fits parse   U. S. Census
        1840 Russell Co KY, William Wilbourn household. Roll

+	41	i.	Acquilla	b 1794
+	42	ii.	Thompson	b 1803
+	43	iii.	*William*	b 1805 KY

8. Samuel Welborn [2] **(James** [1]**)** b c1770, d 183x, m
?Rachel 1ˢᵗ wife 1770-179x by Findagrave. Census indicates he
remarried.
Another of James' sons, & a /s/ of the 1792 petition (footnotes 4 & 42),
he accompanied the Family to KY. In Rowan Co he was a grantee of
Abbotts Creek land from his father, selling that land in 1804 to his
brother William (who stayed in Rowan Co). He was enrolled in the
Rowan [1800]. The KY records are in both Barren, Logan,
Cumberland, & Russell Cos.[47]

Children of Samuel [2] & ?

+	44	i.	Samuel (Jr)	b 1790
	45	ii.	*Jesse*	b c1795
	46	iii.	*James*	b c1809 [48]

132, p32, 12ᵗʰ from bottom. Age 30-40.

[47] U. S. Census
1810 Barren Co KY, Samuel Wilbourn household. Roll 5, p46(43), line
16.
1820 Cumberland Co KY, Samuel Wilbourn household. Roll 19,
p159(136), line 4.
1830 Russell Co KY, Samuel Wilbourn household. Roll 41, p122, 5ᵗʰ
from bottom. Next to James 20-30 & Jesse 30-40.
      1800 Logan Co KY tax list, Jackson R.V., Kentucky
Census, 1810- 1870 (sic); from Ancestry.com Operations.
      The Cos are all contiguous or proximal. Apparently a
large land owner.
Findagrave #7732062. Original stone. Rachel buried Davidson Co NC

[48] both are included on the census listing [1830] above, next
to Samuel– & both fit his [1810 &1820] parse.

9. Joshua Welborn [2] **(James** [1]**)** b 1780, d 1866, m Rachel Smith. Joshua was not in the list of sons of his father, as both he & his brother John were not yet born. Following his Family to Barren Co KY he acquired 200A in 1804. He was the executor of his father's 1811 will. In the census: [1810] in Barren Co; [1820] thru [1850] in Monroe Co KY. The latter gives his age as 70, with Rachel 67 (b 1783). The date of death, 1866, is from FamilyTree– apparently there is no burial record..[49]

Children of Joshua [2] & Rachel [50]

+	47	i.	William	b	1799
+	48	ii.	Joshua Jr	b c1804	
+	49	iii.	Jacob	b c1809/10	

10. John Welborn [2] **(James** [1]**)** b 9/1786, d 7/1824, m Lydia Teague 7/1786- 8/1866 in 1802. The Family bible record includes complete information on vital, m, & issue. The Family remained in Rowan (Davidson) Co throughout. Burial of both was in Davidson Co's Wallburg Cemetery– Findagraves #15403930 & # 7733504 both with original-looking stones. Although he lived until 1824, there is no census– he did /s/ the 1792 petition. (Footnote 42)

Children of John [2] & Lydia Teague Welborn.[51]

50	i.	Margaret	m Anson Payne

---

[49]   Sutherland, James F., Early Kentucky Landholders, 1787-1811. GPC 1986, from Book 10, p521.
FamilyTree/ Ancestry.com verifed by U. S. Census 1850 Monroe KY, Joshua Wilborn household. Roll 213, p429A, family 900. age 70.

[50]   parse: [1810] 2 daus 1800-1810. [1820] 2 sons 1810-1820, 2 sons 1794-1804 & 3 daus 1810-1820 & 2 daus 10-15, 16-25.

[51] All issue is in Family History Library Catalog , FHL US/CAN Film 18067, item 3, p54.
Also see North Carolina Estate Files, 1663-1979, Davidson Co, FamilySearch.org

	51	ii.	Martha	b 1806 d 1880 unmarried
	52	iii.	Isabel	b1808 d 1880 m Alfred Hayworth
+	53	iv.	James M.	b 1812
	54	v.	Rebecca	b 1813 d 1883 m Samuel Edwards
	55	vi.	Choicy	b 1816 d 1886 m Morris Meredith
	56	vii.	Abagail	b 1818 d 1877 unmarried?
+	57	viii.	John	b 1820
	58	ix.	Lydia	b 1823 d 1900 m James Edwards

Generation 3

15. Isaac Jr .[3] (Isaac [2], James [1]) b 1806, d >1880, m Jemima   Matkin, b 1814 in KY, in MO, date uncertain. Regular census [1830 to 1880] St Francois Co MO. The [1830] with his cousins James, William, & Thomas (all of James Jr B2). Issue.[52]

16 Moses Jr. [3] (Moses [2], James [1]) b 1782, d 1826 see Moses discussion above, pps 73,4.

17 Anna. [3] (Aaron [2], James [1]) b c1780, d Feb 1845, m Jacob Duckworth in 1802. Burial in Hopewell Baptist Church cemetery, Anderson Co SC. Findagrave #28206655 with new stone (as Annie).

18 James [3] (Aaron [2], James [1]) b 1784 NC, d 185x in Jackson Co GA. In [1840] his listing is next to Gideon age 30-40;

---

[52]   U. S. Census St Francois Co MO
1830 Isaac Welborn household. Roll 72, p420 (with Thomas, Samuel, & James.
1840 Isaac Welburn household. Roll 230, p64, line 13.
1850 Isaac Wilborn household. Roll 413, p201A, family 690.
1860 Isaac Welborn household. Roll 645, p134, family 657.
1880 Isaac Welborn household. Roll 715, p511B, family 18.

Aaron 20-30; & William 15-20 almost certainly his sons.[53]

19 Thomas [3] **(Aaron** [2]**, James** [1]**)** b 1789, d 1868, m Mary Polly Martin in 1810. All records are in SC. Census [1800, 1810, 1820]. He left a Will in 1868 in Pendleton Co.[54]

20. Ruth [3] **(Aaron** [2]**, James** [1]**)** b 1793, d 1854, m William Duckworth. Findagrave #26345538, burial Ashley Co AR.

21. Aaron [3] **(Aaron** [2]**, James** [1]**)** b 1793? d 1853, m Lucy Stevenson. War of 1812 veteran records SC, lived 1830-1850 in Jones MS. There are two Findagrave records with biographical information and photos of memorial stones from two different cemeteries. The biography in each contains essentially the same information (some of the text is identical): his birth in Oct of 1793 in Anderson Co SC; the move to Jones Co MS; and his military record. The two differ, however, in the date of death and the burial location– one in MS, the other in AR. This difference must indicate

---

[53]   U. S. Census Jackson Co GA
1840 James Willburn household, Roll 44, p 30, lines 19-23.
1850 James Wilborn household, Roll 74, p 260, family 387. Age 66 b NC; wife Eliz. 67 b SC. Son William next door.

[54]   Findagraves #s 9696919 & 9696933; his stone is modern, hers original. The attached biographical information appears correct.
        U. S. Census
1800 Pendleton Co SC, Thomas Wilb?? household. Family #841, p160.
1810 Edgefield Co SC, Thomas Wilbourn household. Roll 62,p45, line 10. Co adjacent to Pendleton.
1820 Pendleton Co SC, Thomas Wilbourne houswhold. Roll 120, p205, line 15.
        Will in Alexander, V., C.M. Elliot, & B. Willie, Pendleton District and Anderson County South Carolina Wills, Estates, Inventories, Tax, and Census Records. Southern Historical Press , Easley, 1980.

some Family history that needs documentation. [55]

22. _Elisha³_ (Aaron ², James ¹) b c1794 d?
This son is included on the basis of a parse & a SC census that places him next to Aaron. There is also an interesting record from AR Territory of Elisha Welborn mentioned in an 1821 memorial to the President regarding Choctaw property. The Territorial Papers of the United State, vol 19, p386.[56]

23. _Gideon ³_ (Aaron ², James ¹) b 1801, d ? m Martha (= Patsey) Elzey b 1797 d 1888. Her burial was in the Cave Springs Cemetery, Lawrence Co AL. Martha also, as widow, in the [1870] Winston Co AL. The only record found linking Gideon to Aaron is a FamilyTree one. Although the Findagrave record gives Martha the link to Gideon, no evidence is visible on the stone. No census has been found for him.[57]

---

[55]   War of 1812 Service record; W.O. 16-581 & 14-294. Two Bounty Land records. Widow Lucy Welborn. Accessed Ancestry.com Jan 2013.
        U. S. Census
1850 Jones Co MS, Aaron Welborn household, Roll 334,
p123A, family 117. Age 56 b SC, Lucy wife.
        Findagrave #s 26627548 (AR) & 13496128 (MS)

[56] U. S. census
1810 Pendleton Co SC, Elisha Wilbourn household. Roll 61, p158A.
Age group 1784-1794 & next to Aaron.

[57]   Findagrave #28863194, Cave Springs Cemetery,
Lawerence Co AL. The stone looks original & readable, but no spouse is apparent.
        U. S. Census
1870 Winston Co AL, Martha Welborn household. Roll 45, p542A,
image 788. Age 70, b NC. The children all b GA.

24. Younger [3], (Aaron [2], James [1])   b 1805, d >1880 m Eliz.? (= Betty); both b SC. Named after his mother's maiden name. He moved with his brother Aaron to MS, recording census there in [1840 thru 1880]. Surviving the Civil War, he served in the 7th Reg., MS Infantry.[58]

25. Samuel [3] (William [2], James [1])   b 1790, d 1869, m ?Catherine Clinard 1794- 1841 in 7/1810. Findagraves #17625975 & 17625863. His stone shows dates & longevity only: hers, no stone & the indicated spouse (Samuel) is 'calculated'. Census records [1810, through 1850] place him in Rowan & Davidson Cos until 1840 when he moved to Guilford Co.[59]

---

[58]   U. S. Census
1840 Jasper Co MS, Y. Welborn household. Roll 214, p182.
1850 Jones Co MS, Younger Welborn household, Roll 374, p123B, family 125.
1860 Jasper Co MS, Younger Wilborn household. Roll 583, p406, family 324.
1880 Jasper Co MS, Y. Welborn household. Roll 651, p127C, line 5. His parent bNC, Eliz.'s bNC.
        U. S. Civil War Soldiers, 1861-1865. database on-line Ancestry.com, 7th MS Infantry (M232, roll 434.

[59]   U. S. Census
1810 Rowan Co NC, Saml Wilborne household. Roll 43, p257, line 12. Age bracket 1784-1794.
1820 Rowan Co NC, Samuel Wilburn household. Roll 81, p320, line 27. Age 1775-1794.
1830 Davidson Co NC, Samuel Wilborn household. Roll 120, p246, line4. Age bracket 1780-1790.
1840 Guilford Co NC, Saml? Welbourn household. Roll 361, p259, line 6. Age bracket 50-60.
1850 Guilford Co NC, Samuel Welbourn household. Roll 632, p260B, family 81. Samuel 59 b Davidson Co: Rachel 64 b Davidson next door, family 80. Note that although the enroller gave the Co of birth (in this census only) Davidson Co was not formed until 1822. We believe his intent was clear. The age brackets are consistent with b 1790.

In [1850] he was a widower, age 59, with issue. Next to him is Rachel, age 64 b Davidson Co 1786 – her identity is uncertain. It is possible she was the wife of one of Samuel's brothers, or an unmarried Welborn. Examination of the former does not produce a candidate, suggesting the latter. Why she had no previous census is a problem.

26. Cary [3] **(William** [2]**, James** [1]**)** b 1792, d 1841. This person is listed as issue of William & Prudence in the Family bible with the notation 'never married'. Is the name male or female? In other W- Families, the name is male. No census can be found.

27. Davis [3] **(William** [2]**, James** [1]**)** b 1792(1796), d 1867, m Hannah Haworth in 1816. Davis was b in Rowan Co, lived there until c1840 whence he moved west to Madison Co IN. Burial was in the Welborn Cemetery in Madison Co. There is uncertainty in his d o b as different sources give different dates. The [1850] has his age as 58 (1792)– the Findagrave as June of 1796. The [1830] fits either. He is not listed in the Family bible, and as such must be assigned parents. In [1820] he is one row from a Joshua of the same age. The [1830] finds him near two widows, Lydia b 1780-1790 & Elizabeth same age group- they are in adjacent rows. Assuming they are Family B3, there should be then two deceased < 1830 males. If the Joshua was his brother, a possibility for one of two widows is as his wife– his only record is the [1820]. No second candidate appears in the records herein, so the problem remains to be solved.[60] All the

---

[60] Findagrave # 36464576– there is no stone or grave site.
   Marriage record– to Hannah Haworth, 1816. NCDAH 02 455.
   U. S. Census
1820 Rowan Co NC, Davis Willburn household. Roll 81, p308, line 4. Age bracket 16-18, Joshua same age, line 6.
1830 Davidson Co NC, Davis Wilborn household. Roll 120,p244, line 3rd from bottom.

information here points to Davis as being of Family B3. Only the fact that Prudence's maiden name was Davis, & the juxtaposition with his cousin Joshua would assign him to William & Prudence (as another son not included in the Family bible – see Moses discussion above).

28. _Moses_ [3] (William [2], James [1]) b 11/1782, d 8/1820(1826) m? Census [1810, 1820]. There are two Findagraves differing only in the death date (footnote 15). He spent his entire life in Rowan Co. The assignment of this Moses to William & Prudence is explained above. We note here that with Davis, two of the four (missing) issue of that pair mentioned in the Family bible are identified.[61]

29. Thomas [3] (William [2], James [1]) b c1808, d ?   The Family bible lists him as the first-born of William & his 2nd wife Rachel Payne– and that he went west to IL. Two census in that State allow a guess at a d o b that the bible record omits.[62]

1830 Davidson Co NC, Elizabeth Welborn household. As above, line 7th from bottom. Lydia Welborn next door. Both age bracket 1780-1790.
1850 Madison Co IN, Davis Wilbourn household. Roll 158,p34, family 480. Hannah 53 bNC.
1860 Madison Co IN, Davis Welborn household. Roll 277, p362, family 976. b 1797.

[61] U. S. census
1810 Rowan Co NC, Moses Wilborne household. Roll 43, p260, line 7.
1820 Rowan Co NC, Moses Wilburn household. Roll 81, p318, line 40.
    Family History Library Catalog , FHL US/CAN Film 18067, item 3, p173.

[62] Family History Library Catalog , FHL US/CAN Film 18067, item 3, p173
    U. S. Census
1840 Cass Co IL, Thomas Willman (sic) household. Roll 56, p36, 9th from bottom. Age group 30-40.
    1855 IL State census. Age group 30-40. IL State Archive, Roll 2192, line 3. (Ancestry.com).

30. Barabas[3] **(William**[2]**, James**[1]**)**   b 11/1812, d 1874, m Jemima Hitchcock in 1834. Census [1840 1850].[63]

31. Wisdom[3] **(William**[2]**, James**[1]**)**   b 1816, d 1881, m Rachel ? Moved west to KY, thence to IL. Census [1870, 1880][64]

33. Isaac P.[3] **(William**[2]**, James**[1]**)**   b 1822, d 1864, m Mary Esther Nichols. The youngest of Williams'. There is no Findagrave file, but a photo of a modern stone in Springhill United Methodist Cemetery, Yadkin River, Rowan Co, found in Ancestry.com FamilyTrees. Census [1850] with Mary & issue.[65]

34. Moses[3] **(James**[2]**, James**[1]**)**   b 1786, d 1834, m Sarah Halbert.1791-1871. The SC Moses discussed above. Findagraves

---

[63]   Vital information from Reeves, Henry & Mary J. Davis Shoaf, comps. Davidson County, North Carolina Will Summaries. By authors, Lexington NC, c1979, p20.
     Marriage: Guilford Co; NCDAH 03 472.
     U. S. Census
1850 Davidson Co NC, Barnabas Wellborn household. Roll 628, p259, family 546. b 1813 NC.

[64]   U. S. Census
1870 Morgan Co IL, Wisdom Wilburn household. Roll 263, p614, family 35. Wisdom b1817NC, Rachel b1818KY.
1810 Morgan Co IL, Wisdom Welborne household. Roll 238, p228B, family 79.
     Findagrave #107836739: no photo, date d 12/1881 only.

[65]   U. S. Census
1850 Guilford Co NC, Isaac Welborn household. Roll 632, p262B, family 14. Isaac b Davidson Co age 28; Mary b Guilford age 27.

#9697062 for Moses & #9697059 for Sarah, modern stones for both. The attached biography for Moses includes his grandparents as parents. Census [1810, 1820, 1830] all Pendleton & Anderson Cos SC. Footnotes 19 &20.

35. Aaron [3] **(James** [2]**, James** [1]**)** b 179x, d ?, m ? This Aaron is identified by inclusion in his father's Will, along with his brothers & one sister. (footnote 40). The [1840] in Ripley Co MO is the only census record found.[66]

36. Thomas [3] **(James** [2]**, James** [1]**)**   b 1803, d 187x, m Susan ?. Accompanied his father to St Francois MO & appearing in [1830 through 1860].   Along with his siblings, he is mentioned in his father's Will (footnote 40). [67]

37. James [3]**, (James** [2]**, James** [1]**)**   b 1804, d ? In his father's Will (footnote 41), & apparently to AL– [1850] ? [68]

38. William [3] **(James** [2]**, James** [1]**)**   b 1798, d 1867m, m

---

[66]   U. S. Census
1840 Ripley Co MO, Aaron Webborn (sic) household. Roll 229, p338, line 1. Age class 40-50, wife 20-30.

[67]   U. S. Census St Francois MO
1830 Thomas Welborn household. Roll 72, p420, line 14.
1840 Thomas Wilborn household. Roll 230, p63, line 20. Carter & Chapley nearby.
1850 Thomas Welborn household. Roll413, p198A, family 655. Thomas 47 bSC; Susan 43SC: issue.
1860 Thomas Welborn household. Roll 645, p135, family 664. Thomas b1803 SC; Susan b1805 SC.

[68]   U. S. Census
1850 Talladaga Co AL, James B. Wellborn household. Roll 15, p400A, family 420. Age 44 b SC; wife Martha 44. His age fits in with those of his brothers.

Nancy Waddell 1800-1868. He was b in SC, and apparently did not accompany his Family to MO. Census [1820 thru 1860] Pendleton to Anderson Cos. He & Nancy have Findagraves.[69]

39. Chapley [3] (James [2], James [1])   b 1808, d ? m ? He was in the Will of his father (footnote 40). There is one court record in St Francois Co MO, before moving to IL [1850] & back to MO [1860].[70]

40. Carter T.[3] (James [2], James [1])   b 1811, d 188x An involment in court cases with his brother Chapley and [1850, 1860, & 1880] comprise his records.[71]

---

[69]   U. S. Census
1820 Pendleton Co SC, William Wilbourne household. Roll 120, p226.
1830 Greenville Co SC, William Wilborn household. Roll 172, p341, line 11. Age group 30-40.
1840 Anderson Co SC, Wm Wellborn household. Roll 507, p146, line .
1860 Anderson Co SC Reg. 42, William Wilborn household. Roll 1212, p322, family 1050. Wm 62SC, Nancy 60SC.
        Findagrave #9696372 (Wm), #9696374 (Nancy); both Memorials, Big Creek Cemetery, Anderson Co SC.

[70]   Aug 1840, Court granted L/T (?) to Chapley Welborn in matter of will of I. Bressie. Saint Francois County Records, pub by Mountain Press, Signal Mountain TN, 2006, p11.
        U. S. Census
1840 St Francois Co MO, Chapley Welborn household. Roll 230, p63, line 12 (im 130- Ancestry.com decodes as 'Chapeen' ?
1850 Calhoun Co IL, Chapley Willborn household. Roll 99, p311A, line 1. b 1808 SC, widower w/issue.
1860 Iron Co MO, Browers household. Roll 624, p657, family 272. Now w/Mary 36 bTN.

[71]   1840 St Francois Co MO, Carter T. Appointed secretary intestate will. Saint Francois County Records pub Mountain Press, Signal Mountain TN, 2006, p22.

41. Acqilla [3] **(Gideon** [2]**, James** [1]**)**   b 1796, d 1864, m Eliz. Wilson in 1816 KY. Born in NC he moved first to KY with the Family, then ~ 1840 to Jackson Co AL. The given name produced a number of interesting spellings in the Census. A Findagrave in Jackson Co gives his d o b as 1794.[72]

42. Thompson [3] **(Gideon** [2]**, James** [1]**)**   b 1803, d ? m Priscilla ?. Enrolled with brother Acquila in [1830]. In [1860] he & Priscilla were in Monroe Co KY.

43. _William_ [3] **(Gideon** [2]**, James** [1]**)**   b c1805, d ? William is included on the basis of a parse fit, along with his brothers Aquilla & Thompson. No census has been found.

44. Samuel jr [3] **(Samuel** [2]**, James** [1]**)**   b 1791, d 1869, m?

U. S. Census
1850 St Francois Co MO, C. T. Welborn household. Roll 413, p199A, family 664.
1860 Stoddard Co MO, Carter (Castor) Welborn household. Roll 657, p384, family 209. b 1810SC.
1880 Stoddard Co MO, Elizabeth Harty household. Roll 737, p601A, family 237. Noted as b 1820 & blind.

[72]   Kentucky Marriages, 1785-1979: FamilySearch, FHL mfilm 209749. "Aquilar Welborn and Elizabeth Wilson, 05 Feb 1816; citing Barren, Kentucky".
        U. S. Census
1830 Barren Co KY, Quiller Wilburn household. Roll 33, p132, line 2nd from bottom. with brother Thompson 3 lines up.
1850 Jackson Co AL, Geviller Wilburn household. Roll 7, p115B, family 162. b 1796NC, Eliz. 1795NC.
1860 Jackson Co AL, Acquila Wilborn household. Roll 11, p277 family 61.
        Findagrave #97537856; 1794-1864. No stone or Memorial. Brief bio mentions parents & cites military record, War of 1812, in KY, 3rd Reg't KY Militia. The AL land was a bounty reward. Burial in Trenton. Eliz's Findagrave #59297809, Jackson Co AL.

Born in Davidson Co NC he moved to Guilford Co about 1835.
Census [1830, 1840, 1850] & a Findagrave. His wife unknown– he
was a widower in [1850].[73]

45. James [3] (Samuel [2], James [1])
46. Jesse [3] (Samuel [2], James [1])

These two sons are assigned Samuel as a result of parsing Samuel's
[1810 & 1820] in KY, and the [1830 & [1840] for James, & [1830
only] for Jesse. Both b 1800-1810.[74]

47. Joshua (Jr.) [3] (Joshua [2], James [1]) b c1804, d ?
m?

The only census appears to be [1820] in Rowan Co, although his
Family was in KY at the time. Joshua Sr in [1800 Rowan] had one
son b 1790-1800. In [1820 Barren Co KY] Sr had three b 1800-
1810. The parse can assign the latter to William b 1799, Joshua jr b

---

[73]   U. S. Census

1830 Davidson Co NC, Samuel Wilborn household. Roll 120, p246,
line 4.
1840 Guilford Co NC, Saml? Welbourn household. Roll 361, p259.
Age 50-60, wife 40-50, five daughters.
1850 Guilford Co NC, Samuel Welbourn household. Roll 632, p260B,
family 81. Son Phillip, daughters Prudence & Catherine. Next door to
Rachel age 64 b Davidson, a cousin.
            Findagrave #17625974; good stone, added info lists seven
daughters.

[74]   U. S. Census

1830 Russell Co KY, James Wilbourn household. Roll 41, p122, 4th
from bottom. He is next to his farther and brother Jesse.
1840 Monroe Co KY, James L. Welborn household. Roll 120, p256,
line 15.
1850 Russell Co KY, James Wilbourn household. Roll 217, p231A,
family 292. Age 41 (1809) b KY. Monroe Co formed 1820-Russell in
1826. Cos contiguous.

c1804, & Jacob b 1809 – consistent through both census footnote 50. There are, apparently, no further records.[75]

48. Jacob [3] (Joshua [2], James [1])   b c1809, d 187x, m Francis A. Griggs in 12/1853. Census 1850 thru 1870. The [1850] record is his father's in which he is listed in the household as age 40[76]

49. William [3] (Joshua [2], James [1])   b 1799, d 187x, m Elizabeth ? b 1802 VA. William was enrolled from [1820] thru [1870] all in Monroe Co KY. In [1840] he is on the same page as Joshua, John, & Margaret (Peggy)– see discussion above; page 70 & footnote 9.[77]

---

[75]   North Carolina County Marriages, 1762-1979. Guilford Co. Facsimile of Bond application, Ancestry.com on-line database.
    U. S. Census
1820 Rowan Co NC, Joshua Willburn household. Roll 81, p1. Both age group 16-26, indicating he had a wife. For Joshua Sr census see footnote 67.

[76]   U. S. Census Monroe Co KY
1850 Joshua Wellborn household. Roll 213, p429A, family 900. Wife Rachel 67NC, Jacob 40KY.
1860 J. S. Welbourne household. Roll 388, p121, family 353. F. A. 23 bKY.
1870 Jacob S. Wilburn household. Roll 593, p133B, family 154. Jacob 60 bKY, Francis A. 55 bKY.
    Marriage 12/1853 in Monroe Co KY. Jacob S. Wilborn, spouse Francis A. Griggs, age 34. Ancestry.com Marriage records on-line database. Original KY Dept. for Libraries & Archives.

[77]   U. S. Census Monroe Co KY
1820 William Welborn household. Roll 25, p115, lines 10,11,12.
1840 Will Wilburn household. Roll 120, p253, same page as Joshua, John, & Margaret.
1850 Wm Wilbourne household. Roll 213, p423A, family 811. b 1799NC.
1870 William Welborn household. Roll 489, p235A, family 31. b 1799;

53.   James M. [3] **(John W.** [2]**, James** [1]**)**   b 1812, d 1882, m Sarah Horney in 1834. James Madison Welborn & his brother John are referenced in the Family bible– see #10 above. He remained in Davidson Co & in census [1840, 1850, thru to[1880]. Both he & Sarah have Findgrave records.[78]

57.   John [3] **(John W.** [2]**, James** [1]**)**   b 1820, d 1874, m2 Rebecca Charles;   Mary Eliza Payne.   There are two Findagrave records– for John & Mary Eliza. Some FamilyTree contributions claim, w/ no documentation, yet another m to a Ms Polly Leonard Imis. As did his brother James M., he spent his entire life in Davidson Co. Census in [1850, 1860, & 1870]. Burial was in the Abbotts Creek Primitive Baptist Cemetery.[79]

Elizabeth 68VA, Eliza 30KY & issue.

[78]   The marriage to Sarah Horney; NCDAH 03 742 on the 9th Feb 1834.
        U. S. Census Davidson Co NC
1840 James M. Willborn household. Roll 359, p264, line2.
1850 James M. Wellborn household. Roll 643, p229, family 107. b 1812NC; Sarah b 1818.
1880 J. M. Welborn household. Roll 961, p224, family 6. Both his parents bNC.
        Findagrave #7733546. Original stone. Family Links correct.

[79]   The m to Rebecca is recorded in the Family bible: Family History Library Catalog , FHL US/CAN Film 18067, item 3, p54.
        Findagrave #15403932 for John T. M. (?) & #15050693 for Eliza. The stone is still readable w/ inscription " w/o Jno H. Welborn Esq., d/o Dr. C.L. & M. A. Payne, ae 25y" Burial was in the Lexington City Cemetery, Davidson Co. John's Family Links are correct, but do not mention a wife. Apparently there is some confusion over his middle name.
        U. S. Census Davidson Co NC
1850 John Welborn household. Roll 628, p257, family 257. He is b

FAMILY C WILLIAM WELBORN Progenitor

Précis of Family C- descendants of William & Hepzebah Stearns
Wellborn (through three generations).

Generation 1

Founder William Wellborn[1] was born in Maryland 1733;
married Hepzebah Stearns/Starnes in 1757; settled in what was to
become Randolph County in about 1756; moved to Wilkes County
NC in 1784/5 and ultimately to Wilkes County GA, where he died in
1792 leaving a Will.

His Will and a Family bible entry allow a record of the issue
of William & Hepzebah numbering thirteen (twelve to adulthood).
The Family Bible entry contains a list of the children, with d o b's,
and some marriages & deaths; Isaac, Elias, Samuel, William (Jr),
James, Clara, Mary, Johnson, Hepzabah, Abner, Nancy, Chapley, &
Wilkes. In his 1792 Will he acknowledged his five youngest;
Johnston, Abner, Nancy, Wilkes, & Shapley. His executors are sons
Isaac & William.[2] Of this issue, all but one, James, accompanied

---

1815; Mary (Eliza Payne) b 1813.
1860 John Wilborn household. Roll 895, p432, family 70. Mary 48
(1812). Issue.
1870 John Welborn household. Roll 1134, p182A, family 125. A large
family.

[1] The double-ll spelling is characteristic of this Family, & is
very consistent.

[2] Family History Library Catalog , FHL US/CAN Film 18067,
item 3.
The Will in Davidson, Grace Gillam, Early Records of
Georgia, vol 1, 1932. Pub. by Rev. Silas Lucas jr., Vidalia GA in 1968,
p68.
Curiously, the TXDAR lists two Marys; one b 1770 d 1776

William to Wilkes Co GA.

Among the earliest NC records for William is a 1764 Court filing of a land transfer from Thomas Wilburne (Progenitor of Family A) to William of 120A, with H. Husbands a witness. He also /s/ the 1771 petition in support of Thomas, accused of being one of The Regulators.[3] These records show evidence of mutual cooperation amongst the early W-s not presently determined to be related. One son, James, 1767-1853, remained in the Granville District, marrying twice and leaving eleven Generation 3 offspring, all noted in the second Family C Family bible.[4] The other sons & daughters of William & Hepzebah moved to Wilkes County GA with their parents. The Georgia genealogical material should be consulted for those descendants not included in the Formal Genealogy below.

The marriage of William to Hepzabah Stearns (Starnes) occurred in 1757. She was the daughter of Isaac Stearnes and wife Rebecca Johnson. Both spellings are given in the bible with the supposed intent of either being interchangeable or that the bible

---

with a Mary b 1778 & m Nicolas Wiley. The Family bible's Mary lived only six years and there is no record of a 'replacement Mary'.Texas Society of the DAR, The Roster of Texas Daughters of Revolutionary Ancestors, vol. 4, 1976 in Texas (sic).

[3] Weeks, Eve B., trans, Register of Orange County, North Carolina Deeds- 1752-1768 & 1793. Heritage Papers, Danielsville GA, 1984, p30.
CRNC v9, pps 23-26.

[4] The original bible of James C2 is/was in possession of Nancy M. Welborn of Surry Co. The bible of William is/was in the possession of Mrs J. S. Welborn of High Point N.B. the dates of the DAR transcription of the Family bibles is not known-See References Appendix Two.

author(s) were unsure of which was correct.[5]   Material available on Ancestry.com suggests that the early 19th Century variable surname spellings that were characteristic of many families applied here as well.   In the Families the variable name appears:

• C3 of Isaac, given name Stearns as recorded by the TXDAR;
• B4 of Acquilla: son Starnes census [1850 - 1880].

Generation 4 is not included in this Chapter;

• B3s of James & Rebecca: Rachel Starnes Wellborn, m N. Cannon (bible); Nancy M. m Dr Saml Stearnes (bible) or Starnes (Findagrave #11867571 for Rebecca– added information).

In general, examining the NC bibles without regard to The Families, both spellings occur– there is some doubt that separate families with both surnames occurred in the region, but with considerable doubt as to the consistency of their use.

Generation 2

Family C2 James was born in Nov of 1767 ; married Rebecca Montgomery b Oct 1762 in 1794: this couple produced nine children. All are listed in the Family bible with other records to verify the entries. Rebecca d 1860 in Marshall Co MS, moving there as a widow to be with her daughter Rebecca Franklin.[6]   James had a military career and was referred to as 'Colonel' and later as

---

[5] E g Shubal Stearns, Baptist minister of Sandy Creek, Randolph Co, www.northcarolinahistory.org. Rebecca Stearnes Polk, NCGJ Consolidated Index, vii, p183,on p 514 of Index. Entry of four NC Starns in NCGJ Consolidated Index; Isaac, Charles, & Peter Starnes 1779 tax list Randolph Co., Compiled Census & Census Substitutes Index, 1790-1800; Ancestry.com on-line database. Census Population schedules: [1790] 4 Starns; [1800] 10 Starns , one Starnes; [1810] two Starns, six Sterns.

[6] Vital data is from the bible, footnote 2; the only record of Hepzebah b 1812 is also in The Family bible.
        Findagrave #11867571 w/original stone & very good biographical information.

'General'. In addition, James served in the NC Senate from 1796 to 1811.[7]

In his Will, he mentions his wife, Rebecca; sons, Samuel C., H. M. (Hugh M.), & granddaughters of those two sons. The two sons are listed as executors.[8]

FORMAL GENEALOGY

Generation 1

1. William Wellborn [1],   b 1733 in MD d 1792 in GA, m Hepzebah Stearns in 1757. William's first record in NC is a grant in Orange Co (Chapter One, p4). He very probably was a customer of John McGee's Ordinary, recorded as a debtor in 1773. (See p10, Chapter One). The first Wilkes Co GA record was in 1784– a grantee of 200A on Long Creek.[9]

The children of William [1] & Hepzebah

+	2	i.	Isaac	b 1758	
+	3	ii.	Elias	b 1759	
+	4	iii.	Lucy	b 1761 m Benj. Barton 1779	
+	5	iv.	Samuel	b 1763	

---

[7] Wheeler, John H., Historical Sketches of North Carolina 1584-1851, v II, p 466. Hickerson, Thomas F., Happy Valley (The Yadkin Valley) History & Genealogy. by author, Chapel Hill NC, 1940.

[8] Rowan County Will Book5; folio 118, Abstract in The Rowan County Register,v7(3), p1602.

[9] The NC record: MARS 12.14.95.267.

McGee's Ordinary: NCGJ 1(1), p38ff.

Davidson, Grace Gillam, Early Records of Georgia, vol 1, 1932. Pub. by Rev. Silas Lucas jr., Vidalia Ga in 1968, p238-9. Many of William's records are contained in Davidson's two vols, including his 1792 Will, footnote 2.

+	6	v.	James	b 1767	
+	7	vi.	William	b 1765	
	8	vii.	Clara	b 1768	m James Dennan
	9	viii.	Mary	b 1770	(No records)
+	10	ix.	Johnson	b 1772	
	11	x.	Hepzebah	b 1774	(No records)
+	12	xi.	Abner	b 1776	
	13	xii.	Nancy	b 1778	m Nicholas Wiley
+	14	xiii.	Chapley	b 1780	
+	15	xiv.	Wilkes	b 1780 (twins) [10]	

Generation 2

2. Isaac [2] (William [1])   b 1758, d 1839, m Mary Barton 1760-1848. Isaac accompanied the Family to Wilkes Co GA. He is a DAR Patriot for his service in the Revolutionary War (in John Hind's Company)– a biography given in White's Abstracts. The Pension Roll of 1835 also records him.[11] While his first apparent record in Wilkes Co GA is for a 1794 tax, there occurs a gap of some twenty-odd years before his records begin in Madison Co AL. The

---

[10]   The order here is that in the Family bible: the order in the Roster of Revolutionary War Soldiers of GA is different & does not include Lucy, Nancy, Hepzebah &, inexplicably, Wilkes (he d 1796, see below). The TXDAR list includes all including Wikes, with no additional information. For two of the daughters, there are no records found. A FamilyTree record cites a m record for Hepzebah w/out a reference.

   Roster reference is McCall,Mrs Howard H. comp., Roster of Revolutionary Soldiers in Georgia, vol 1. Clearfield Reprints (GPC), 1996 (Original 1941). The TXDAR ref is The Roster of Texas Daughters Revolutionary Ancestors, Texas Society of the National Society, Texas 1976. p2249-50.

[11]   White, Virgil D., Index to the War of 1812 Pension Files, vol iii. National Historical Publishing Co., Waynesboro TN, 1989. White's Abstracts, p3736. White mentions pension applications by Isaac Jr & daughter Levicy.

first AL census in 1830 records him. [12]

His death in 1839 & burial in a Patriots grave is given in Hatcher.
Mary is recorded in [1840] Madison Co AL.[13]

The children of Isaac [2] & Mary[14]

+	16	i.	James	b c1780
+	17	ii.	Elias	b 1792
+	18	iii.	Isaac (Jr)	b c1800

---

[12] 1794 tax, Blair, Ruth, Some Early Tax Digests of Georgia.
GA Dept. Archives & History, 1926-reprint 1971, p296.

1816 Madison Co, MS territory Residents list; AL
Compiled census & substitutes list, Ancestry.com on-line databse. Orig
R V Jackson AL

U. S. census
1810-1890. U. S. census 1830 Madison Co AL Isaac Wilbourn
household. Roll 4, p79, line 13. Both Isaac & Mary age 70-80 w/one
male 5-10!

[13] Hatcher, Patricia Law, Abstract of graves of revolutionary
patriots, Vol 4, S-Z. Heritage Books, Westminster, MD. 2007 ed,
p172..
Findagrave #65496809 as Isaac Starnes Wellborn.

U. S. census
1840 Madison Co AL, Mary Wellborn household. Roll 13, p141, line
19, age class 50-60; one female 20-30.
Mary Welborn, widow of Isaac, received pension payment thru
Nashville TN Office, 1835-1850. Ancestry.com on-line database;
original Ledger of Payments etc, National Archives Microfilm Pub.
T718, facsimile in author's archives..

[14] This list is partially taken from The Texas DAR reference
The Roster of Texas Daughters Revolutionary Ancestors, pub Texas
1976, p2251. This record omits #16 James entirely– the evidence is
given in his Formal Genealogy record.

U. S. census
1830 Madison Co AL, Isaac Wilbrum (sic) Sr household. Roll 4, p79,
line 13. age class 70-80, one male 5-10 !.

+	19	iv.	William	b c1784
+	20	v.	Stearns	b 1783
+	21	vi.	Shelton	b ??
	22	vii.	Nancy	m Henry King
+	23	viii.	Levicey	b 1781
+	24	ix.	Polly	b ??

3. Elias [2] (William [1]) b 1759, d 1836, m Mary Marshall
Although accompanying his father to GA, he is not in the Will – The
Family bible does, however, include him with a note of his m. After
a single record in Wilkes Co NC, he was enrolled in [1830]
Columbia Co GA where he was buried. As with his brother Isaac, he
served in John Hind's unit in the Revolutionary War, & is listed in
the Pension Roll of 1834.[15]

The children of Elias [2] & Mary[16]

	25	i.	Ruby	b? m Dr. Davis
+	26	ii.	Marshall H.	b 1798
+	27	iii.	Stephen	b c1794
	28	iv.	Lucy Morrow	b? m1 G. Lewis, m2 ?

---

[15] Revolutionary War Pension & Bounty-Land Warrant
Application Files, 1800-1900. Widow's Pension Application by Mary,
1834. Ancestry.com database-on-line. Original M804, Roll 2526, 67
pps.
     List of Captain John Hind's Company, 1780; RCGJ xxxi
(3), Fall of 2007, p21. This was a militia unit.
     U.S. census Columbia Co GA
1820 Elias Wellborn household. Roll 7, p42,line 13.
1830 Elias Wellborn household. Roll 16, p361, line 1.
     Findagrave #95523981. good DAR bio, taken from
Whites's Abstracts 3736.

[16] This list from McCall, Mrs Howard, comp, Roster of
Revolutionary Soldiers of Georgia, vIII. Clearfield reprint 1996 (1941),
p177. It appears to be complete. See Generation 3 for census parse.

+	29	v.	James Madison	b c1785
	30	vi.	Martha	m Wm Briscoe
	31	vii.	Selina H.	m Theo. Hill
	32	viii.	Mary	m ? Fleming
+	33	ix.	Abner W	b c1775
	34	x.	Nancy	m Nat. Bailey

4. Lucy [2] (William [1])   b 1761, d ? m Benjamin Barton 10/1779. A facsimile of the marriage bond document allows the following information: William & Isaac Welborn are witnesses to the Condition of Obligation by Benjamin Barton who has applied for marriage to Lucy Wilburn. William & Isaac must be Lucy's brothers. [17]

5. Samuel [2] (William [1])   b 1763, d 1822, m Mary ?. Col. Samuel, as he was known, does not appear in his father's Will. He is recorded as participating in The Cherokee Wars, presumably from his d o b as in the Eastern TN conflict 1776-1783. The first GA record is a land acquisition in 1792. [18] Col. Samuel left a non-cupative will in 1822, the Estate administered by his wife Mary. [19] There is no [1820].

The children of Samuel [2] & Mary

---

[17] FamilySearch.org, North Carolina County Marriages, 1762-1979. Image 407 of 1301 in 004364150.

[18]   fold3 #311336076: Co Three, NC militia. Davidson, Grace Gillam, Early Records of Georgia, vol 1 p 78., 1932. Pub. by Rev. Silas Lucas jr., Vidalia Ga. 1968. 200A, Clark's Fork of Long's Creek.

[19]   His heirs are listed: Chas R Greene, John W. Wellborn, Katherine C. Wellborn, Mrs. Wellborn, later Mrs Jock Smith. Quinn, Sarah, Early Georgia Wills & Settlements of Estates; Wilkes County. Clearfield Pub., 2003 (1959), p24.

+	35	i.	Samuel Jr	b	?
+	36	ii.	*John W.*	b	?

6. James [2] **(William** [1]**)**   b 1767,   d 1854,   m Rebecca Montgomery 1776-1860 in 1794. This son, the only one to remain in NC, has many records (22 in The DataBase, some referred to above). He & Rebecca had eleven children & accounting for them contributed more to the total. He was enrolled in all census [1800 to 1860] ! [20]   Rebecca's Will lists heirs R. S. Cannon (#38),. R. N.(sic) Franklin (#40), E. A. Ledbetter (= Betsey #44), & son William W. (#37). [21]

The children of James [2] & Rebecca[22]

---

[20]   U. S. census Wilkes Co NC (examples)
1800 James Willborn household. Roll 33, p68, line 9. age class 26-44.
1830 James Willburn household. Roll 74, p358, line 9. age 60-70.
1850 James Wellborn household. Roll 656, p336, line 14. age 82 bNC.
      A brief biography appears in The Rowan County Register, v7(3), 1952, p1602. More in Hickerson, Thomas F., Happy Valley (The Yadkin Valley), by author, Chapel Hill, 1940.

[21]   Rebecca Findagrave #11867571. Burial Early Grove Cemetery, Marshall Co MS, beside her daughter Rebecca W. Franklin. Original stone still readable- all issue listed correctly. A source in The NCGSJ, v4, #3, p153 on British Claims includes in a brief biography of her father Capt. Hugh Montgomery, mentions his two natural daughters, not named, but m to Montfort Stokes and ___ Welborn in Wilkes Co.
      James' Will, Book5, folio 118, dated 5/1853; Rebeccas' Book 5, folio 273; both abstracted in The Rowan Co Register v7(3), 1992, p1602.

[22]   Family listed in FHL US/CAN Film 18067, item 3, p39.
Marriages of two of the daughters have been recorded:
Rachel S. to Col Newton Cannon of TN is in e g The Raleigh Register for Nov 13, 1818; fide Broughton, Carrie, L., Marriage and Death Notices in Raleigh Register and North Carolina State Gazette 1799-1825, GPC, Baltimore, 1975, p87. This record needs editing as it gives her name as Raphael- probably handwriting.

+	37	i.	William	b 1799
	38	ii.	Rachel Starnes	b 1795 m H. Cannon of TN.
	39	iii.	Nancy M.	b 1797 m Dr Samuel Stearns.
	40	iv.	Rebeccah M.	b 1801 m Bernard Franklin
	41	v.	Lucy B.	d early of burns.
	42	vii.	Katherine S.	b 1806 d 1829 m ? Parks.
+	43	viii.	James J.	b 1808
	44	ix.	Betsey A.	b 1809 m Wm Ledbetter (=Eliza)
	45	x.	Hepzebah M.	b 1812 (no records)
+	46	xi.	Samuel C.	b 1816.
+	47	xii.	Hugh M.	b 1816 (twins)

7. William ² (William ¹)   b 1765, d 1822?, m Lucy Moore.

William Jr presents some difficulties as his records are few & possibly confused with other Williams– see Chapter Two. A GA militia record, War of 1812, is probably his. The Family bible says b 1765, m Lucy Moore 1819 in Wilkes Co GA, but if so at age 54. Additional records would be welcome.[23]

8. Clara ² (William ¹)   b 1768, d ?, m ? Dennan in FL.

Daughter Nancy M. m to Samuel S. Starnes. NC Marriage records Ancestry.com on-line database; image 5514 of 6376 of bond, July 1816.

[23]   fold3 # 310346808, 4t Regt (Booth's) GA militia. Davidson, Grace Gillam, Early Records of Georgia, v2, p398. Repub. by Rev. Silas Lucas jr., Vidalia GA, 1968. FamilyTree says d 1822 w/no reference.

9. Mary [2] **(William** [1]**)**   b 1770, d 1776. bible record only.

10. Johnson [2] **(William** [1]**)**   b 1772,   d 1822,   m Sallie Render. As Johnston in 1790 reconstructed census.[24] He was a Justice or Judge of a Wilkes Co GA Court.

The children of Johnson [2] & Sallie
+   48   i.   Johnson Jr.   b 1794 [25]

11. Hepzebah [2] **(William** [1]**)**   b 1774, d ? m ? bible record only.

+   **12. Abner** [2] **(William** [1]**)**   b 1776, d 1842, m Patsey Render 1776-1842 in July of 1810. Served in the 1812 GA militia, 38th Battalion as Commander. Enrolled in [1830]. His will /s/ in 1835 mentions children, but only Wilkes Welborn named. The Estate record, however, includes daughter Hepsiba [sic]. [26]

---

[24]   1790 reconstructed census-- De Lamar, Marie & Elizabeth Rothstein, The Reconstructed 1790 Census of Georgia. GPC, Balt., 1985.

U. S. census
1820 Wilkes Co GA, Johnson Willborn household. Roll 9, p163, line 2.
As Justice, fold3 image #18328543.
Davidson, Grace Gillam, Early Records of Georgia, 1932.
Pub. by Rev. Silas Lucas jr., Vidalia Ga. In 1968. v1, pp136-; v2, p309.

[25]   U. S. census
1830 Houston Co GA, Johnson Willborn jr household. Roll 18, p261.
1850 Barbour Co GA Johnson Wellborn household. Roll 1, p109A, family 20. Age 56 b GA, Elizabeth 30.

[26]   fold3 #24021445, name only on payroll record.
1835 Will in Smith, Sarah Quinn, Early Georgia Wills & Settlements of Estates; Wilkes County. Clearfield Pub., 2003 (1959), pps 34,58.

13. Nancy ^{2} (William ^{1})   b 1778, m Nicholas Wiley

+   **14. Chapley R. ^{2} (William ^{1})**   b 1780
+   **15. Wilkes ^{2} (William ^{1})**   b 1780

Information on the twins is from largely undocumented FamilyTree. That e g from a Milledgeville Newspaper giving details cannot be verified with newspaper searches. A search for Wilkes produces nothing solid: Chapley (Ross) does have an 1808 tax list record in Franklin Co GA as well as a m record.[27] Presumably a son, Chapley H., has Ancestry.com records.

Generation 3
16. James ^{3} (Isaac ^{2}, William ^{1})   b c1780, d ?,   m ?
This James is included among the issue of Isaac & Mary Barton Wellborn on the basis of two AL census [1830] & [1840] in which he is listed on the same page (each) with his siblings Isaac (Jr) & Elias. In the former, their father is also listed, age class 70-80.[28]

1790 GA reconstructed. Land lottery of 1819.
   U. S. census Wilkes Co GA
1830 Abner Willborn household. Roll 21, p306, last line.
1840 Abner Wellborn household. Roll 53, p273, line 18.

[27] Tax record, Ancestry.com Operations data-base on-line. Original from R.V. Jackson, Georgia Census, 1790-1890.
   A marriage to Nancy Sloan appeared in a Georgia Pioneers Genealogical Magazine, vols 20-22, p34. (Accessed Google Books, May 2015.)

[28] U. S. census Madison Co AL
1830 Isaac Wellborn Sr household. Roll 4, p79, line 13.
   James Wellborn household. Roll4, p78, line 15.
   Isaac Wellborn household. Roll 4, p 78, 3rd bottom age class 20-30.
   Elias Wellborn household. Roll 4, p 78, 2nd bott. age class 30-40.
1840 Elias Wellborn household. Roll 13, p119, line 11 age class 40-50

17. Elias [3] **(Isaac** [2] **, William** [1]**)**   b 1792,   d >1860,   m2 Ann Tillman in 12/1821 Madison Co AL: [1860] lists his wife as Elizabeth. The History of Jackson County, Alabama   has brief biography of this Elias. Deceased 11/1865, heirs listed, but no wife acknowledged. Sons Joshua, George W. James L. & William S.: daughters Tabitha Sublett, Vina Maples. [29]

18. Isaac [3] **(Isaac** [2]**, William** [1]**)**   b 1783, d 1851,   m ? see brother James, above.[30]

19. William [3] **(Isaac** [2]**,William** [1]**)**   b c1784,   d ? The only record is believed to be an 1811 tax role in the Indian

----

James Wellborn household. Roll13, p119, line 20, age class 50-60. (Inexplicably, Ancestry.com lists this entry as Jas Welstead– there is no problem with the handwriting.)

This son is not included in the TXDAR list of Isaac's son. There is evidence that all of Isaac2's Family lived in AL.

[29]   M record is in Ancestry.com Marriage Collection (database-on-line, multiple original entries).

Kennamer, John R., History of Jackson County, Alabama. Press of Southern printing & publishing Co.,1935. Filmed 1939 by Gen. Soc. of Salt Lake. The facsimile excerpts available on Ancestry.com are from vol 17 & vol 19 containing Will information: d 12/1864.

U. S. census Madison Co AL
1830 Elias Wellborn household. Roll4, p78
1840 Elias Wellborn household. Roll 13, p119, line 11 wife 30-40. , same page as his brother James Wellbourn, age 50-60.
1850 State census, AL Dept of Archives & History, Ancestry.com on-line database. Age >45, issue.
1860 Jackson Co AL, Elias Wilburn household. Roll 11, p441, fam 704. age 68 bNC, Elizabeth 60 bNC.

[30] U. S. census, footnote above.

Findagrave #138869316- there is no stone photo & burial location unknown. Vital information from DAR.

Lands & Madison Co of AL.[31]

20. Stearnes [3] (Isaac [2], William [1])   b 1783,   d 1851
This son is listed by the TXDAR & is a calculated addition to Isaac
C2's Findagrave (as Isaac Starnes Wellborn). As well, there is an
Isaac Starnes Jr 1783 - 11/1851 buried in Shelby Co TN. There are no
available records on Ancestry.com suggesting that the burial record
is family history and/or DAR accounts. However, there is a record
which clearly points to a Generation 4 Stearnes, not 3.[32]

21. Shelton [3] (Isaac [2], William [1])   Only a single record is
available.[33]

23. Levicey [3] (Isaac [2], William [1])   b 1781,   d 1849,   m
Robert Davis or Davie. This daughter applied for Pension relief,
the only issue of Isaac C2 to do so.[34]

---

[31] William Wilborn, AL 1810-1819 Tax Lists Index, Indian
Lands: AL 1811-1819 Tax Lists Index, Madison Co. Both from
Ancestry.com Alabama, Compiled Census & census Substitutes Index,
1810-1819, on-line-database. Original R.V. Jackson, Alabama Census,
1810-1890.

[32] Findagrave #138869316 for Isaac S. Jr, no stone, parents
as Isaac S. & Mary.

[33] Shelton /s/ a 1822 petition in AR territory. Papers of The
United States, v19, p400, family #12. fide ANC.com Ops
         Findagrave #65496809 for Isaac lists sibling Shelton as m
Paulina Murray.

[34] Findagrave #126956892. 9/1781- 9/1849, burial Hazel
Green, Madison Co AL. wife of Robert Davie as 2nd wife. Issue.
         There is a fold3 document 1849 Madison Co AL in which
/s/ Levicy Davies applies for pension relief. A facsimile is available
under her Ancestry.com search.

24. Polly [3] **(Isaac** [2]**, William** [1]**)**   This daughter is, apparently, a mystery– was she a daughter of Isaac? She appears in [1830 AR] with children. As Shelton was in AR territory in [1820], above, it is possible that she was 1) the widow of Shelton, or 2) unmarried with Shelton's issue.[35] So much of IsaacC2 & Mary's issue is difficult to document using Ancestry.com. This branch of The Family has no known bible– it is possible that the TXDAR list was contained in an unpublished one.

26. Marshall H [3] **(Elias** [2]**, William** [1]**)**   b c1806, d ? Parsing the [1820] & [1830] results in, first, three b 1804-1810; thence two b 1800-1810. A satisfactory fit for the three: Marshall, Abner, & James M., the latter two (below), his brothers. Marshall married twice & acquired property in Warren Co GA about 1878.[36]

---

[35]   1830 AR Territory Polly Wilbourn household. Roll 5, p242, line 8. age class 40-50; w/five males, oldest 20-30 & one or two females <5. Ancestry.com lists this entry as Pally Williams– there is no problem w/handwriting. There is also a 1830 tax list record, Pulaski Co. Ancestry.com on-line database.

[36]   A marriage record for Marshall M. (sic) Welborn to Frances M Hardaway, 8/1841 in Warren Co GA. Ancestry.com, GA Marriage Records From Select Counties, 1828-1978. on-line database, 2013.
      Findagrave for Elias, #9552398, says Marshall Hampton m Adaline Hill.
      McCall, Mrs Howard H. comp., Roster of Revolutionary Soldiers in Georgia, vol 1. Clearfield Reprints (GPC), 1996 (Original 1941) lists both, p 177.
      Georgia Property Tax Digests, 1793-1892. Ancestry.com Operations, image 807/840.
      U.S. census 1850 Warren Co GA, Marshall H. Wellborn household. Roll 86, p161B, fam 529. age 42 bGA, Francis M.? 30 b GA.

27. Stephen [3] **(Elias** [2]**, William** [1]**)**   There are no records found. Possibly [1820] GA Wilkes Co, Stevens (sic) Wellborn. Roll 9 p187 line8. b 1775-1794.

29. _James Madison_ [3] **(Elias** [2]**, William** [1]**)**   b c1807, d ? m Louisa Cody.[37] One of a number of James Madison W-s: it is difficult to keep them all straight; but see parse result above.

33. Abner W. [3] **(Elias** [2]**, William** [1]**)**   b c1810, d ? No certain records on Ancestry.com can be found. There is a Civil War record (Ancestry.com) for a A. J. Welborn, CSA Co H, 26th Inf. Batt. that might be him. He fits the parse for Elias, above.

35. Samuel [3] **(Samuel** [2]**, William** [1]**)**   There is a single record that points to this son– a mention in father Samuel's Estate that a debt of Mary (his wife & Executrix) was paid by Samuel Jr.[38]

36. _John W._ [3] **(Samuel** [2]**, William** [1]**)**   b ?   d? He is an heir of Samuel's 1822 GA Will, but there are no clear GA records. It is possible he was a cousin– John B3.

William [3] **(William** [2]**, William** [1]**)**   The Family bible includes his father (#7.) with a m to Lucy Moore. If we accept a FamilyTree record of the m occurring in 1819, then if William Sr his age would have been 54; if Jr the m age would be more to be expected. He must also be included in the plethora of Generation 3 Williams. (See Chapter Two, Part Two) & Chapter Four.

---

[37] Biography on Elias Findagrave #95523981 gives m Louisa Amanda Cody, & as son of Elias, both attributed to DAR.

[38] Davidson, Grace Gillam, Early Records of Georgia, v2, 1932. Pub. by Rev. Silas Lucas jr., Vidalia GA in 1968, p78..

37. William [3] **(James** [2]**, William** [1]**)** b 1799, d >1850, m Anne Perkins Franklin in 1823. Moved first to TN, thence to MS. Also known as William Wilkes. A Gibson Co TN deed in 1836 contains the following: William W. Wellborne made & entered an indenture with Newton Cannon & William Ledbetter in favor of William W.'s father James of Wilkes Co NC, etc. Note that N. Cannon had m William's sister Rachel (#38); & Wm Ledbetter was very probably the husband of his sister Betsey (#44)[39]

39. James Johnson [3] **(James** [2]**, William** [1]**)** b 1808, d 1828 Died young & without issue. As a result he is not in his father's Will. The Family bible does include him. His death notice was in The Raleigh Register, Friday, 23 Nov., 1827, p3. Information from Findagrave #86304703. Burial in the Welborn Cemetery, Wilkesboro.

46. Samuel C. [3] **(James** [2]**, William** [1]**)**   b 1816, d 1856
47. Hugh M. [3] **(James** [2]**, William** [1]**)**   b 1816, d 1865
The twins were b in 1816. Samuel C. m Mary Stearns of TN & d 1856. FamilyTree lists two m; Mary Elizabeth Starnes & Mary Chapley. As the only census, [1850] ([1840] is missing) gives his wife as simply Mary b1825 TN, & the m i 'C' presumably stands for Chapley, the available material does not allow an answer. There is a Findagrave record with no stone, but including correct Family material.
Hugh Montgomery (also as H.M. in the Will) m Nancy Martin & has

---

[39]   U.S. census
1840 Shelby Co TN, William Wellborn household. Roll 211, p530, line 20.
1850 Marshall Co MS, William W. Household. Roll 377, p 310, family 442. Age 51, Ann P. 45 bNC.
Gibson Co TN Deed Book F, p417-8: fide contributed FamilyTree transcription, available Ancestry.com. census [1840] Shelby Co TN; [1850] Marshall MS.

a good Findagrave record. [40]

[40]   U. S. Census Wilkes Co NC
1850 Samuel C. Welborn household. Roll 649, p236A, family 1267.
Age 34NC, Mary 25TN. W/ parents- James & Rebecca & yr-old
daughter Rebecca J.
1850 Heigh (sic) Wellborn household. Roll 649, p 269B, family 276.
Nancy 29 b Wilkes Co.
Findagrave #86256491, Samuel Chapley Wellborn, burial Wellborn
Cemetery, Wilkes Co.
Findagrave #86198064, Hugh Montgomery Wellborn, no stone photo,
but good Family biographies. burial in Martin Cemetery, Wilkes Co
NC.
As brothers they obtained Warrants & Plats in Wilkes Co NC from
1833-1835. MARSid 12.14.124.3584.

FAMILY D   JOHN WELBORN   Progenitor

Précis of Family D- descendants of John & Sarah York Welborn..

This Families' founder is placed in Generation 2 to keep the early chronology aligned. John 1754-1805 could well have been the son of another Generation One North Carolinian, but much more work must be done to establish that this is so.

The move West to KY, OH, & IN, instead of to the South, left a single Generation 2 son in Randolph Co.

Founder John poses something of a problem owing to the multiplicity of early Granville John W-s. To distinguish John D2, reference should be made to Chapter Two, Part One. Note, however, that all the problems associated with that complex have not been resolved. John's death in 1805 mitigates these difficulties somewhat– he could not have been one of the four [1810] Randolph County Johns (p 17).

John left a will (or wills) in 1805/1806 and an Estate in 1808.[1] The Will mentions six sons & four daughters– one son not mentioned in the Will (James) died at age 15, and is included in the Family bible reference. Wife Sarah, née York, is also included. In the Estate proceedings sons John b1792, Isaac b 1793, & Enoch b 1797 are designated as minors, and their subsequent histories are in the formal genealogy below

Generation 3

The most interesting of John & Sarah's sons, in this author's

---

[1] Family of John 1754-1805 & Sarah York m 1773 in Family bible: Family History Library Catalog , FHL US/CAN Film 18067, item 3,p 171.   Will see below.

opinion, is Jesse York Welborn. Born in December of 1779 in Randolph Co NC, he moved as a young man to KY and thence to Posey County in Indiana's toe. Chronologically, he was b 12/1779 in Randolph Co NC, remained there through at least 1805 & 1806; moved to KY sometime before 1812 where he was a Volunteer in the War of 1812, serving in the 4th Regt (Mounted) of KY Volunteers. He then moved across the Ohio R. to Posey Co IN, his arrival there in 1814 recorded by Dorrel.[1] He is mentioned, prominently, in two History references recording his move from KY and his affairs in Posey County. He d in August of 1835, but left no known Will.

There is no marriage record (in either NC, KY, or IN), but it is certain that his wife's name was Elizabeth. Her maiden surname is provisional. According to FamilyTree her name was Elizabeth Warren Crabtree (1790-1850), but apparently without hard record.[2]

---

[1]   U.S. War of 1812 Service Records, 1812-1815. Roll Box 226 of M602: Ancestry.com on-line-database.
Dorrel, Ruth, Pioneer Ancestors of Members of The Society of Indiana Pioneers. Indiana Historical Society, Indianapolis, 1983, p231. note; she incorrectly assigns Jesse a d o b of 1788.

[2]   The entire family sheet containing information does not seem reliable. Her name is given as Elizabeth Waren Crabtree b 11/1790 in Hillsboro NC, daughter of James Crabtree. There was, in fact, a James C. in Hillsboro Co in [1810] with a daughter of correct age. Ostensibly, in support, a Wm Crabtree was a partner of Jesse Y. in an early hotel venture in Posey Co about 1820. (Wheeler, John, H., Historical Sketches of North Carolina, 1584-1851. GPC (Clearfield) 1993 (1825)). It seems likely that the FamilyTree submitter used that fact; went searching for a NC Crabtree that fit; and found one. Moreover, this sheet assigns the birth state of three of Jesse's sons as NC- 1800 to 1830- whence he & Elizabeth were clearly in IN. While the evidence for assigning Jesse' Elizabeth to a Crabtree might be persuasive, it must be considered circumstantial because no marriage record has been found in either NC or KY. The Ancestry.com source pedigree sheet is labeled as 'Griffith-Holloway-Mitchell-Welborn'

Now to the determination of the children of Jesse Y & Elizabeth Welborn. Census data reveals the first problem– accounting for the Family makeup living with Jesse Y. and Elizabeth. No KY census data exist: in Posey Co IN census is available in [1820 & 1830], with [1850] for Elizabeth– no [1840] can be found, but see below. The principal puzzle is the identity of the two males in Jesse's age class in the [1820]. The first credible hypothesis would be that the two were Jesse's siblings. As the three youngest siblings could not be in this age class, the two that could would be William b 1777 and Elias b 1781. So where were these two in 1820? Elias was, without question, in Preble Co. OH; and William, according to the evidence, never left Randolph Co. NC. (See the Formal genealogy below.) We simply do not know who these men were– the import below is the question of the census composition– were they Jesse's or a mix?

Two of their children are given by the [1850] in Posey Co IN: Elizabeth was enrolled with George W. age 23 b IN, & Enoch E. b 1834 IN. The remaining issue must be established, if possible, using a parsing of [1820 & 1830] Posey Co schedules, and a list of residents of Posey & surrounding counties.

TABLE FIVE   Parsing the age distribution of the children of Jesse Y & Elizabeth Welborn from the Schedules, Posey Co IN.

[1820]		males		females	
<10	1810-1820	2	William W. 1819	Jesse H. 1818	1	Polly A*
10-15	1804-1810	1	John C. 1808		1	?
(16-18)	1801-1804					
16-25	1794-1804	2	Joshua 1799	?	1	?
26-44	1775-1794	3	Jesse Y 1779	? & ?	1	Eliz.

* b 1814-1817 FamilyTree data

[1830]   males   females

<5	1825-1830	2	George W. 1827	?			
5-9	1820-1825	1	James C. 1824*			1	Marie L. 1822
10-14	1815-1820	2	William W.	Jesse H.			
15-19	1810-1815					1	?
20-29	1800-1810	2	Joshua	John C.			
30-39	1790-1800					1	Eliz. 1790
40-49	1780-1790						
50-59	1770-1780	1	Jesse Y				

* Will Posey Co 1859.

Note that Joshua, William W. & Jesse H. repeat. If we assume the [1820] to be a combined Family, only a missing son b1825-1830 in [1830] remains unidentified.
In support: William W. [1850] Posey Mt Vernon, b 1820, p175 near Eliz. Will Posey Co 1878.

Jesse H. [1850, 1860, 1880] Henry Co IN. d o bs 1821, 1818 (2), 1816. parent b NC.

John C. [1840] b 1800-1810 ?1863 CSA 14th NC Inf. possibly returned to NC to fight for the Confederacy.

James C. based on Will only, no census found.

Joshua records in Wayne & Henry Cos (Court & land) [1840 thru 1870] Henry Co Atlas. Henry, Spiceland near cousins Elias & Emsley. b 1799/1800 in NC. [3]

---

[3] Census support for these sons is given in the Formal Genealogy below.

These are considered sons of Jesse Y & Elizabeth. The daughters' information comes from FamilyTree.

FORMAL GENEALOGY

Generation 1 [4]

1. John Welborn [1], vital data   b 1754, m Sarah York in 1773, d 1805 leaving a Will. His heirs listed; Sarah, his wife, Ann White, William Welbourne, Jesse Y. Welbourne, Elias Welbourn, Martha, Elizabeth, Sarah Welborne, John Wilbourn, Isaac Wilbourn, & Enoch Welbourn.[5] Following John's death, Sarah remarried Elias Cowan, & son Jesse petitioned the Court on behalf of minors John, Isaac, & Enock to benefit from any real estate prescribed in the Will; Sarah having voluntarily relinquished her rights. He was taxed in 1803 along with sons Elias & William. Census in [1790 & 1800] [6]

---

[4]   In this Formal Genealogy the Generations are calculated from the earliest progenitor, in keeping with suggested practice. The above Generation assignments are in keeping with Table One, Chapter One.

[5]   All from Family bible. Will in Randolph Co Will book 3 folio 27/28. (author has copy). Note the surname spellings– the handwriting is somewhat faded, but mostly translatable. Sarah Wilbourn & Jesse Y Wilbourn testators. Nov term 1805.

[6]   RCGJ IV(4), p12: the original, North Carolina Estate Files, 1663-1979, index & images, Family Search, images 00966 to 00974, see 00969. Also on FamilySearch: North Carolina Probate records, 1735-1970; Wills Cross Index, 1793-1902, vol 01, image 147. Shows devisees of John, 1805, as Elizabeth, John, Isaac, & Enoch. 1803 tax, RCGJ XI(1), pps 5,6, 1987, Captain Duncan's District-
1803 Randolph County Tax List, Capt Jones District. ibid, pps 5-7.
U. S. Census Randolph Co NC
1790   John Wilborn dist. 1/3/5. Roll 7, p28.
1800   John Wilborn household. Roll 32, p347, line 20.

Children of John [1] & Sarah

	2	i.	Ann	b 1776	m ? White
+	3	ii.	William	b 1777	
+	4	iii.	Jesse Y	b 1779	
+	5	iv.	Elias	b 1781	
	6	v.	Martha	b 1784	m Isaac Wright
	7	vi.	Elizabeth	b 1786	=?Elizabeth Ann
	8	vii.	Sarah	b 1788	no records
+	9	viii.	John	b 1792	
+	10	ix.	Isaac	b 1793	
+	11	x.	Enoch	b 1797	

Generation 2

3.   William [2] (John [1]) b 1777, m Hulda ?, d 185x.
Census for William, all Randolph Co where he spent his entire life,
[1800, 1830, 1840, 1850, & possibly 1810][7] The 1803 tax list
includes him, with his brother Elias & father John. footnote 6.
The [1850], Randolph Co, has him next to his son Levi, with wife
Hulda. There are, apparently, no land acquisition records for him, &

---

[7]   [1810] is a bit of a puzzle as the age distribution includes a
male b <1766., as well as 1765-1784 that would point at William. It is
difficult to assign this census to any other Randolph Co William. The
identity of the older person– it need not be a William if the enroller
determined the head of household to be our William.
        U. S. Census Randolph Co NC
1800 William Wilborn household. Roll 32, p351, line 20
1810 William Wilborn household? Roll 38, p 60(184), line 5th from
bottom. Age class distribution: >45 (<1766), 26-44 (1765-1784), 16-25
(1784-1794); females >45, 16-25.
1830 William Wilborn household. Roll 125, p63, line 4. Age class 50-
60 for both Wm & wife. Two daughters
1840 William Welborn household. Roll 369, p88, 9th from bottom.
1850 William Welborn household. Roll 641, p228B, family 942. Age
72, wife Hulda 70NC, next to Levi.

no burial or Estate records.

The children of William [2] & Hulda

+   12   i.   Levi   b 1807

4.   Jesse Y(ork) [2] (John [1])   b 1779, m Elizabeth Crabtree?,
d 1835 in IN.
He was enrolled in [1820 & 1830] Posey Co, and Elizabeth in
[1850]; without a doubt his widow, although no [1840] IN for her
can be found. [8] The difficulty of establishing their issue is described
above.

The children of Jesse Y [2] & Elizabeth

+	13	i.	*Joshua*	b 1799NC	
+	14	ii.	John C.	b 1808NC	parsed
+	15	iii.	Jesse H.	b 1818	
+	16	iv.	William Wallace	b 1819	
			?James C.	b 1824	d 1859
+	17	v.	George W.	b 1827	
+	18	vi.	Enoch E.	b 1834	

5.   Elias [2] (John [1])   b 1781, m2 Elenor Swafford,
Rebecca ?, d 1851 in OH. The m to Elenor (sic) was in Randolph
Co, and after the 1803 tax there (footnote 6) he moved West to OH,
taxed there in 1816.[9] All census [1820 thru 1850] were in Preble Co
with his Will   filed   there in 1851.   Heirs– wife Rebecca, sons
Emsley; Elias decd with heirs Eleanor & Sarah; William decd, sons
George Washington & Henry Harrison; David; & John. Daughters

---

[8]   U. S. Census Posey Co IN
1820 Jesse Y Wilborn household. Roll 13, p305A, line 1.
1830 Jesse Y Welborn household. Roll 29, p172, line 4. Age class 50-
60.
1850 Elizabeth Wilburn household. Roll 166, p176B, family 129. Age
60 bNC. With two sons, George W. b1827 & Enoch E. b 1834.

[9]   Powell,E. W., Early Ohio Tax Records. GPC reprint, p325.

Williber (?) Jones; Eleanor Small; Sarah Brown; Elizabeth Miller, dedc; Margaret Swafford; Deressa Talbert; & Nancy Skinner.[10]

    Children of Elias [2] & (Elenor d 8/1802), Rebecca ?

+	19	i.	Emsley	b c1805	
	20	ii.	Elias jr	b ?	d by 1851 parse only
+	21	iii.	George W.	b 1827	
+	22	iv.	Henry H.	b ?	
+	23	v.	David	b 1815	
+	24	vi.	John M.	b 1834?	

9.   John [2] (John [1])   b 1792, m Barbary Brower, d 185x. m to Barbary (sic) in July 1809 in Randolph Co. Census [1820,thru,1850] Posey Co IN.[11]   Parse for [1830] William 1829, James H. 1811; one 1820-25, 1810-15, 1800-1810; missing 6 fem! For [1840] William repeats; one 1830-35, 1825-30, repeat 1820-25: four females, John a widower.

---

[10]   The daughters do not appear below: see text above for list.

          U. S. Census Preble Co OH, e g

1820 Elias Wilbourn household. Roll 95, p99, line 4th from bottom.

1850 Elias Welborn household. Roll 723, p 266B, family 500. Age 69 bNC, Rebecca 69 bPA.

OH Will Abstracts, vol ii 1836-1854 p27, folio (315). Facsimile from http://interactive.ancestry.com/49305/PrebleCntyWills.

Findagrave #61194889 photo w/readable stone, d Sept 8, 1852, age 71 years. Mound Hill Union Cemetery, Preble Co OH.

[11]   U. S. Census Posey Co IN, e g

1820 John Wilborn household. Roll 13, p357, 2nd from bottom.

1840 John Welborn household. Roll 90, p285, line 15. Age class 1780-1790; no apparent wife.

1850 John Wilburn household. Roll 166, p196, family 411. Age 53 b NC, wife ?Sinara bTN.

Children of John² & Barbara

+	25	i.	James H.	b 1811
+	26	ii.	Joseph	b 1818
+	27	iii.	William	b 1829

10.   Isaac ² (John ¹)   b 1793, m Sarah Burges, d 185x.
In 1805 he was involved in the Probate of his father's Estate. The devisees Elizabeth, John, Isaac, & Enoch. His 1815 m to Sarah NC m records.[12] Census is [1830] in Posey Co IN with no male issue indicated. Apparently moving again, South to Obion Co TN, [1850] with Sarah & sons John & Wm. [1840 missing] [13]

Children of Isaac ² & Sarah

+	27	i.	John B.	b 1831
+	28	ii.	William	b 1833.

11.   Enoch ² (John ¹) b 1797, m2 Jane Baker 1824, Mary Ashbridge in 1841, d 1887.
Enoch, the youngest of John & Sarah York Welborn was b in Randolph Co NC in 1797. He was apprenticed to his older brother Jesse in 1808, as a Jeweler & Silversmith. His first census [1820]

---

[12] Marriage NCDAH 01 289.
1820 tax Grigg, Barbara N. & Carolyn N. Hager, 1820 Tax List, Randolph County North Carolina. Randolph County Historical Society, Asheboro, 1978, p17.

[13]   John's Estate probate 1808, Randolph Co. North Carolina Estate Files, 1663-197, NCDAH.
M to Sarah, NCDAH 01 289.
U. S. Census
1830 Posey Co IN, Isaac Welborn household. Roll 29, p172, line 20. Age class 30-40 with no male issue.
1850 Obion Co TN, Isaac Millburn (sic) household. Roll 891, p347B, family 415. Age 58 bNC?, Sarah 53 bNC. Children b IN & TN. Eldest John 19 William 17

was in Sumner Co TN; the m to Jane Baker was in Davidson Co TN; & census there in [1830, 1840]. In the former, the only issue was a female age 10-15. In the latter, he was alone suggesting that Jane had d. The m to Mary Ashbridge, as Enock, was in TN (no Co stated) in March of 1841.[14] There is a census record in St. Louis MO in [1850] with Mary b 1821 in VA; with his occupation 'watchmaker'– remember the apprenticeship! The [1860] appears missing, but he was in Posey Co IN in [1870 & 1880] as a widower and blind. His d in 1887 is from FamilyTree.[15]

Generation 3

12. Levi Welborn [3] (**William** [2], **John** [1]) b 1807, m Marium Alred in 1825, d 1855. Levi stayed in Randolph Co his entire life, census in [1830, 40, & 50] & leaving a Will in 1855. There are a number of Court records including service on a Grand Jury. Details of the Will

---

[14]   TN State Marriages, 1780-2002; Ancestry.com on-line database, accessed July 2013.

[15]   Apprenticeship, RCGJ XXII(2), p22. Miller, Alan , Middle Tennessee's forgotten children: apprentices from 1784 to 1902. Clearfield, Balt. 2004, p39.
     m to Jane TN Marriages to 1825. ANC ops data-base-on-line access 7/2013.
     U. S. Census
[1830] Davidson Co TN,Enoch Welborn household. Roll174,p301,line7. age 30-40 wife 20-30, 1f 10-15, apparently their only issue & unknown.
[1840] Davidson Co TN, Enoch Welborn household. Roll 520, p271, line 10.
[1850] St Louis MO, E. Wilborn household. Roll417,p59B, fam 631. b 1797, Mary 29VA.
[1870] Posey Co IN,, Enoch Welborn, Greathouse family, Roll 352, p30B, ED101, fam 269.
[1880] Posey Enoch Welborn, living in boarding house. Roll 305, p205B, family 269 Dunlap boarding house. Age 83 & blind.

are found in his Estate file: his executors were his sons William &
John A. Heirs were the sons, wife Marium & a daughter Hulda. [16]

13. Joshua [3] **(Jesse Y.** [2] **, John** [1] **)**   b 1799 in NC, m Phoebe ? d
>1870 in IN. Some of his history is given above in the discussion of
Jesse's issue. His first record in IN was in 1822 in Wayne Co & a
year later was appointed to the Grand Jury in adjacent Henry Co.
Census in [1840,50,60,70] all Henry Co. Phoebe was recorded
[1880] living with a son. [17]

14. John C. [3] **(Jesse Y.** [2] **, John** [1] **)**   b 1808 in NC, m Francis ?,

---

[16]   Cemetery record RCGJ x(1), p39.
Member Grand jury Fall term 1834, RCGJ xxxi(4), p10.
    U. S. Census Randolph Co NC
1830 Levi Wilbern household. Roll 125, p71, line 3rd from bottom. Im
43 of 50. Regiment 2 (Ancestry.com does not recognize this entry).
1840 Levi Welborn Household. Roll 369, p98, line 17.
1850 Levi Welborn household. Roll 641, p228(641), family 941. Here
Ancestry.com has his wife as 'Monone'.

[17]   Dorrel, Ruth & Thomas D. Hamm, Abstracts of the
Records of the Society of Friends in Indiana. Vol 1, revised, Indiana
Historical Society, 1996.
Grand jury from Pleas, Elwood, Henry Co Past & Present,
Knightstown IN, reprint 1967.
M record NCDAH 03 742.
    U. S. Census Henry Co IN
1840 Joshua Wilborn household. Roll 87, p 133, line 14.
1850 Joshua Welborn household. Roll 151, p251, family 12. age 51,
Phoebe 48.
1860 Joshua Welborn household. Roll 266, p181, family 1316?.
1870 Joshua Welborn household. Roll 323, p309A, family 277. Age
70NC, Phoebe 68NC
1880 J.C.T. Welborn household. PhoebaWelborn 77NC. Roll 284,
p227C, family 292.

d ? Only census records– the TX inferred from the m I & parse. [18]

15. Jesse H. [3] **(Jesse Y.** [2] **John** [1])   b 1818, m Martha ?, d 1908 in IN. Census [1850,60,80].[19]

16. William W. [3] **(Jesse Y.2,John1)** b 1819, m Hannah ?, d ? From above discussion of Jesse Y's issue.[20]

17. George W. [3] **(Jesse Y.** [2]**, John** [1]) b 1827, d ? His only record is [1850] Posey Co IN, with his mother Elizabeth footnote 17. Likely, but in need of further research, is a Civil War record for a George W. Welborn in the 60th IN inf as a pvt.[21]. As the Pension File is dated 1879, he apparently survived the War.

---

[18]   U. S. Census
1840 Posey Co IN, John C. Welborn household. Roll 90, p284, line 7th from bottom. Age class 1800-1810.
1880 Denton Co TX, John C. Welborn household. Roll 1300, p8, ED 103, family 6666 !. b 1808NC, Francis 69NY.

[19] d in IN WPA C-4, p5 from Ancestry.com on-line database.
      U. S. Census Henry Co IN
1850 Jesse H Welborn household. Roll 151, p254, family 53.
1860 Jesse Welborn household. Roll 284, p200A, ED 12, family 11. b 1818 IN
1880 Jesse H. Welborn household Roll 284, p200A, family 111 b 1816. Martha 54 bIN.

[20]   U. S. Census
1850 Posey Co IN, William W. Wilburn household. Roll 166, p175, family 111. b 1820IN, Hannah 30OH, listing near to his mother Elizabeth.

[21] fold3, George W. Welborn, pvt Co B 60th IN Inf. im# 249432. Listed as an invalid & with un-named widow

18. Enoch E. [3] **(Jesse Y.** [2]**, John** [1]**)**   b 1834, m Francis Boswell, d 1929! B in Posey Co IN, he resided in Gibson Co IN, in IL's Hamilton, Jefferson, & Washington Cos. He was a physician.[22]

19. Emsley [3] **(Elias** [2]**, John** [1]**)**   b c1808, d ?
Although b in OH, his records other than census are found are in IN. He acquired land in Henry Co in 1833 & 1835, acknowledged as from Miami Co OH. His only census [1840], Preble Co OH, next to his father, b 1800-1810. The chronology here is a bit strange, but the locations are all close. [23]

20. Elias Jr. [3] **(Elias** [2]**, John** [1]**)**   b ?,   m Mary Argbright in 1832 d < 1851. Image copy of the m record is available <www. pcdl.lib.oh.us/marriage > record ID marap251, accessed Oct 2015. B ? & was deceased at the time of his father's Will in 1851. Footnote 10, from Elias' will.

---

[22] M Francis Boswell, Gibson IN, 1853. IN WPA Index, Book 1, p OS367. Ancestry.com on-line database.
    U. S Census
1860 Jefferson Co IL, E. E. Wilborn household. Roll 187, p798, family 69. Age 29 bIN, Francis 26 bIN; occupation physician.
1870 Hamilton Co IL, E. E. Welborn household. Roll 225, p554B, family 50.
1880 Washington Co IL, E. E. Welborn household./ Roll 256, p367D, ED126, family 214.
    Directory of Deceased American Physicians, d 12/1929.

[23]   Mayhill, R. Thomas, Land Entry Atlas of Henry County Indiana, 1821-1849. The Bookmark, Knightstown, 1980. Large 10x13", unpaged. Author has copy- a remarkable work, showing the plats of the land holders.
    U. S. Census
1840 Preble Co OH, Ensby (sic) Wilbourn household. Roll 421, p126, line 21. Next to father Elias as Ellis, age 50-60. The enrollers apparently had a great deal of trouble with the names.

21. George W. [3] **(Elias** [2]**, John** [1]**)**   b 1827, d ? Did he survive?
Can be confused with his cousin of the same name #17.
The separation is due entirely to two different Civil War records: his
cousin, above, in the 60th IN infantry; his in the 35th OH infantry.
George W. Welbourn, Co F, 35th OH Inf. as private.[24]

22. Henry H. [3] **(Elias** [2]**, John** [1]**)**   b ?, d ?.
His only record is as an heir in his father's Will. Footnote 10.
It is possible he was (another) Civil War victim.

23 David [3] **(Elias** [2]**, John** [1]**)**   b 1815, m Mary Jane Hudlow in 1845
d ?
In [1850] he was enrolled in his father's household, age 35. [25]

24. John M. [3] **(Elias** [2]**, John** [1]**)** b 1831 m Delana Beckin d 1898
Census [1860, 1880]. Enlisted Co H, 93rd OH inf. survived Civil
War. John M. Welborn, burial Greenlawn Cemetery, Howard Co IN.
Photo of stone w/Civil War inscription. Gives vital as 8/1834 to
11/1898.? Findagrave #46194507 w/new stone
Parents given as Elias & Eleanor Swafford Welborn.[26]

---

[24] fold3; George W. Welbourn (Wilburn), Co F 35th OH Inf,
image # 296443079.

[25] Dodd, Jordan, Preble Co OH marriages 1803-1900. fide
Ancestry.com on-line database.
1850 Elias Welborn household. Roll 723, p 266B, family 500. Age 69
bNC, Rebecca 69 bPA, David 35 bOH. Mary J. is not listed - her fate is
unknown.

[26] Civil War record: enlisted 21 Jly 1862, age 31 (= 1831) Co
H 93rd OH inf. Mustered out 6/1865 in OH. Official Roster of the
Soldiers of the State of Ohio. Ancestry.com on-line database, accessed
9/2014.
    U. S. Census

25. James H.³ (John², John¹)   b 1811,   m2   Mary Moore 1816-1841; Eliza ? d ?

James along with his brothers fit John's census parsing in [1820 & 1830] with only a son b 1820-1825 unaccounted for. He moved west to MO. [27]

26. Joseph ³ (John ², John ¹)   b 1818, m Nancy Mills, d 8/1897. Although the handwriting on the census schedules leaves his m i uncertain, the burial record in Bellfontaine Cemetery, Posey Co gives his full name as Joseph Franklin Welborn. His place of birth is given as Guilford Co NC– wife's name is also provided. [28]

27. William ³ (John ², John ¹)   b ?1829 IN, d ?

1860 Preble Co OH, John Welborn household. Roll 1026, p159, family 1009. Age 29 (1831), wife Delana 25IN
1880 Tipton Co IN, John Welborn household. Roll 315, p126, ED132, family 213. Age 49 bOH, Delany (sic) 40 bIN his parents bNC.
M nodate, Indiana marriage records, 1850-1920. WPA Book 661.
    Findagrave #46194507

[27]   Finda #11649458, photo original stone.
    U. S. Census Lafeyette Co MO
1870 James H. Welborn household. Roll 240, p768, family 248. Age 59 (1811), Elisa 47 bIN.
1880 James H. Welborn household. Roll 698, p315B, ED053, family 14. Age 68 bNC, Eliza 58 bIN. His parents bNC.

[28]   U. S. Census Posey Co IN
1850 Joseph B. Welborn household. Roll 166, p318B,family 964. Age 32 (1818), Nancy age 30 b unk!
1870 Joseph Welborn household. Roll 352, p249A, family 162. Age 51 b NC, Nancy 48 b IN.
1880 Joseph F Welborn household. Roll 305, p100D, ED097, family 223. Age 62 b NC, Nancy 60 b NC. His parents b NC, her parents b GA!.
Findagrave #66441782. Information on a carved stone of indeterminate age.

The only records that can be ascribed to this son are 1) [1850] Wayne
Co IN. Age 21 (1829) living w/father John (#9) 2) [1860] Wayne Co
IN, age 36 (1824), b IN as William J., living in a Hotel.[29]

28. John [3] (Isaac [2], John [1])   b 1831 IN,   d ?
29. William [3] (Isaac [2], John [1])   b 1833 IN
these two sons of Isaac & Sarah were enrolled in the [1850] Obion Co
TN. See footnote 10 for Isaac #10.

---

[29]   U. S. Census
1850 Wayne Co IN, John Wilburn household. Roll 166, p196B, family
411. William eldest son, age 21.
1860 Henry Co IN, Peden family hotel. Roll 266, p515, occupant 16,
William J. Welborn age 36.

FAMILY E   EDWARD WELBORN- progenitor

Précis.

The first task in the history of this Progenitor & his Family is to establish as near as possible the ds o b. The 1806 Will of Edward Wilbourn of Surry County lists his sons & heirs; Richard,, John, Thomas, Zachary, Lewis, & Edward, jr. Because the Family given names were used in subsequent Generations– not an unusual occurrence– these vital data are of critical importance.[1]

Using census, and some early tax records, the following Table attempts to establish vital data for Edward and his sons. Separating records of Edward Sr & Jr is especially critical.

TABLE SIX
Census Age-class Summary for Edward & Sons

Edward	E1	[1800] Surry Co*	<1756
	E2	[1810] Knox Co KY	<1766
Richard	E2	[1790] Surry Co**	<1775
		[1800] Surry Co	<1756
John	E2	[1800] Orange Co	<1756
Thomas	E2	[1810] Cumberland Co KY	<1766
Lewis	E2	[1800] Wilkes Co	1755-1774
		[1830] Claiborne Co TN	1760-1770
Zachary	E2	[1810] Madison Co KY	<1766

*   See below for estimate
** This census had distribution 4/-/3. The interpretation here is that

---

[1] Will of Edward Wilbourn, Surry Co NC, 1806. Facsimile copy is in the author's archives. Will Book 3, pps 70-72.

census enrolled seven members of Edward's Family, as he was in GA at the time (See below). Richard was apparently chosen as Family Head.

Notes for the Table: not all available census were used. If the age class given did not contribute additional information (e g dates later than those shown) they were not included.[2]

The Will order is apparently not the birth order: from the Table we propose the following; Richard, John, Thomas, Zachariah, Lewis, Edward (Jr). (The last three in any order). All the sons were b <1770.

The d o b of Edward, pére, can be estimated from the Surry County State census taken 1784-1787.[3] The family age distribution

---

[2]   U.S. census
1800 Surry Co NC, Edward Wilborn household. Roll 32, p698. Next to Richard.
1810 Knox Co KY, Edward Wilbourn household. Roll 7, p86(664), line 2
1790 Salisbury (Surry), Richard Wilbourn household. Roll 7, p522, col 3,line 4.
1800 Orange Co NC, John Wilbourn household. Roll 34, p605, line 4.
1810 Cumberland Co KY, Thomas Wilbourn household. Roll 9, p174, line 14.
1800 Wilkes Co NC, Lewis Willborn household. Roll 33, p69, line 2.
1830 Claiborne Co TN, Lewis Sr household. Roll 180, p108, next to Lewis Jr.
1810 Madison Co KY, Zachariah Wilbern household. Roll 7, p235, line 7 of 2nd p.

[3]   Register A. K., State Census of North Carolina 1784-1787, 2nd ed. Rev.. GPC, 1974, p144. Register is not consistent in date-labeling the enrollments–very possibly that was impossible from the original material. Presumably the same information dated 1782, Surry Co is in Ratcliff, Clarence E., North Carolina Taxpayers, vol 2, GPC, 1989. The State census report does not indicate what would result if the senior person was older than 60.!

was a single white male 21-60 years of age; with three white males under 21 (or over 60); and three females. This distribution suggests the older male was father Edward, with three of his sons. Assuming that the record age 21-60 was at the oldest end of the range, Edward Sr could have been b as early as c1724-1726; the latest 1764. As the first Edward records are 1754 - 1762, we take the earliest as nearer the truth.[4]

The next problem is to identify, if possible, the three males less than age 21– in 1784 they would have had to be born after 1763, & combined with the results of Table Five, before 1770. This suggests that the three are the youngest of Edward's.

In summary, then the d o bs for the Generation 2 sons are:

Richard c1753	John c1754	Thomas c1760
Zachary c1763	Lewis c1764	Edward c1765

Generation 1

A Family chronology was constructed– from the 1750s through 1840, including the evolving Counties in the Old Granville District, as well as Georgia & Kentucky Counties. The early chronology for Edward can be blocked rather easily into first; records in the Granville-Orange Counties 1762 to 1778; second, Surry County 1782-1786 & 1800-1822; third, Wilkes County GA 1787-1794.

The Granville-Orange Co records, 1762- 1778, are all land acquisition land & deed transfer ones, but for two very early Rowan Co Court proceedings in which Edward was, briefly, appointed Constable. Ibid He acquired land in Surry Co about 1762

---

[4] 1754 Appointed Constable Rowan Co, & removed 1756, Linn, Jo White, Rowan County North Carolina Abstracts of the Minutes of the Court of Pleas & Quarter Sessions, 1753-1762 (& also 1762-1774, 1775-1789) 3 vols. Pub by author, Salisbury, 1977, 1982. This reference vol 1, p33 from Court II:59.

1762. Land, Sandy Creek, MARS 12.14.95.270. There is an undocumented date of 1728 given by a FamilyTree researcher.

& sold it in 1764. [5]

Records in GA commence in 1784-5 and continue thru 1794. Examination of 1787 deed transfer in Randolph Co NC has Edward of Wilkes Co GA & wife Martha grantors to John Welborn. In 1789 the Wilkes Co GA land records reveal grantee Thomas Jr ; the grantors were Edward & wife Marthew (sic). John is surely their son, but son Thomas has no records in GA; & indeed in that year he was in KY.[6]

---

[5]   Land 1762. There are a number of recordings of this acquisition that probably all refer to the same 425A. MARS 12.14.95.270; Hofmann, Margaret M., The Granville District of North Carolina, 1748-1763; Abstracts of Land Grants, by author, 1987, p100.(From Patent Book 12, 2259, p55). Chain carriers were William & Thos Welborn ! suggesting that the early Welborns might have been related.
Bailey, Pat Shaw, Land Grants Records of North Carolina, vol I Orange County 1752-1885. Pub. by author, Graham N.C., 1990. Land 1763. MARS 12.13.103.15.
    Deed transfer, Nov 1764. Grantor Edward Wilborn of Orange Co 100A Sandy Creek to Edward Cowan same Co. Orange Co Deed Book 3, p 194. Witnesses William & Thomas Welborn. Can be found in Bennett, William D. Ed., Orange County Records, vol 3; By author Rocky Mount 1990,(LOC 1987 Raleigh) p45.

[6]   On list of GA's Roster of Revolutionary War veteran's: Knight, Lucian L., Georgia's Roster in the Revolution. Georgia Dept. Archives & Hist. GPC, 1967, p394.
    1785 deed transfer Davidson, Grace Gillam, Early Records of Georgia, vol 1, 1932.(Pub. by Rev. Silas Lucas jr., Vidalia Ga in 1968), p289. Edward & wife Martha, 95A Clark's Creek, to Thomas Welborn. 1787 Randolph Co NC, Edward of Wilkes GA & Martha grantors to John Welborn. Grigg, Barbara N., Deed Abstracts Randolph County Books 1-5, 1779-1794. By author, no date, p52. Available NCDAH, Raleigh.
1789 Edward & wife Marthew (sic) to Thomas Welborn jr, 230A Greenbier Creek. Davidson G vol2 p126 from Book G-G. Wit: Thos Sr.

The crowd of W-s in & along the SC-GA border from 1772 thru 1792 presents some problems. In 1784 & 1787 Edward acquires headrights to a number of parcels in Greene & Wilkes Cos GA. However, in these latter ones he is also listed with a number of W-s of both Family C & some unidentified. The latter include a Thomas or Thomases; Curtis, Joshua, & Jonathon. (In [1810] Cumberland KY, Thomas E2 w/Robert & Edward were enrolled along with Zachariah. Thus we are assured the KY Thomas is indeed E2.)[7]

From 1772 thru 1792 the Counties involved (Washington & Wilkes Cos GA) were all along the SC-GA border. The foregoing indicate that a family or families of W-s, that included Edward E1, immigrated to newly-opened lands: most did not involve any of them with a NC background.   Again, it is quite possible these W- families & Families were related: the resolution of this question is not within the purview of this Book.

No certain GA records exist after 1789 when Edward & wife Martha deeded 230A on Greenbrier Creek to Thomas.

Finally, he left a Will back in Surry Co NC in 1806. footnote 1 above.

The chronology is interpreted as indicating an individual with interests and residence in multiple places. All are suggestive of a single, but peripatetic Edward.

---

[7]   There are records from Granville Co SC & Greene Co GA for an Edward W-. FamilyTree contributed facsimile Court documents linking these to an Edward Levi Wellborn, although the middle name nor dates appear. The Family E chronology records never include a 'Levi' & it is difficult to place Edward E1 out of Orange & Surry Cos until 1784.
Lucas, Rev Silas jr, Index to Headrights & Bounty Grants, Georgia 1756-1909. Georgia Genealogical Reprints, Vidalia 1970, pps 695-706. Also see Blair, Ruth Some Early Tax Digests.

Generation 2

Some important Family information is given in the 1819 Will of son John E2, who died without issue. The Will lists as heirs his siblings in addition to some nephews & ?nieces. The reference to Lewis clearly refers to his brother: the Daniel, however, is another matter. There is no Daniel in Generation Two– and to which parent we assign him is uncertain. His d o b must be such that in 1819 he was old enough to have family, so certainly b < 1800. No such Daniel fitting this requirement appears in the DataBase, leaving the matter unsolved. Parsing reveals only one possibility– E2 Thomas had two sons b 1784-1794 only one of whom can be identified, Edward. [8]

Generation 3

The given names Edward, Richard, Robert, & Lewis occur in Generations Two & Three requiring some care in assigning parents. An Edward b c1790 was enrolled in [1810] Cumberland Co KY: as both Edward E2 & Thomas E2 moved to KY, Edward E3 must belong to either. Parsing solves this problem as Edward E2 had no sons recorded in age class 1784-1794, whereas Thomas did.
Roberts– there are two. One b c1775, the other 1794. The age disparity might be a problem. Parsing alone suggests the former was son of Thomas (b c1760) and the latter of Richard (b c1753).
The c15 year difference in Thomas-Robert is certainly a problem, but both dates are approximate.

---

[8] A facsimile copy of the Will is in the author's archives. Notable is the fact that R. Shields' abstract omits some of the names. Shields, Ruth H., Abstracts of wills recorded in Orange County, North Carolina 1800-1850. GPC, Baltimore, 1972.

The text in the Will is subject to some interpretation, see Formal Genealogy below.

FORMAL GENEALOGY

Generation 1

1. Edward Welborn [1], vital data b c1728, d 1806, m Martha ? First records are in Rowan & Orange Cos (1754 - 1769), the latter on land of Sandy Creek with other W- Progenitors. Capt. William Bueford's Militia Unit, 1771, included Edward Wilborn, Corporal. In 1778 he declared oath to the King from the Nap of Reeds District, Orange Co. About 1785 he began acquiring land along the SC-GA border. In 1784/1785 military service & deed transfer place him in Wilkes Co GA. [9]

He & Martha remained there until 1794, returning to Surry Co NC where his Will was probated in 1806. (footnote 1) The [1800] has him in Surry Co next to his son Richard. [10]

---

[9]   1771 Militia, Colonial Records of North Carolina; Roster of the Granville County Militia, vol 22, pps 160-167.

May 1778, Oath taken before Robt. Harris, Nap of Reeds District. /s/ Edward Wilburn. E g http://docso.uth.unc.edu/csr/index.html/document/csr22-0042.

1784 Edward on list of Georgia's Roster of Revolutionary War. Knight, Lucian L., Georgia's Roster in the Revolution. Georgia Dept. Archives & Hist. GPC, 1967, pzz.

1789 deed transfer Edward Welborn & wife Marthew (sic) to Thomas Welborn Jr, 230A in Greenbrier district. Davidson, Grace Gillam, Early Records of Georgia, vol 2, 1932. Pub. by Rev. Silas Lucas jr., Vidalia Ga in 1968. Deed Book G-G, p 126.

1794 tax Wilkes Co Ga. Ibid, p 14. Also in Blair, Ruth, Some Early Tax Digests of Georgia. GA Dept. Archives & History, 1926-reprint 1971, p30.

[10]   U. S. Census

1800 Surry Co NC, Edward Wilborn household. Roll 32, p698, line 2. Age class <1756

The children of Edward [1] & Martha:[11]

+	2	i.	Richard	b c1753
+	3	ii.	Jane	b ?
+	4	iii.	John	b c1754
+	5	iv.	Thomas	b c1760
+	6	v.	Zachary	b c1763
+	7	vi.	Lewis	b c1764
+	8	vii.	Edward	b c1765
	9	viii.	Temperance	b ? m Marshall as of 1806
	10	ix.	Susannah	b ? m Jones as of 1806
	11	x.	Lida (=Lydia?)	b ? m Slaughter as of 1806.

Generation 2

2. Richard Welborn [2] (Edward [1]), b c1753 d c1802, m Susannah Roberts.

The only census records are the [1790], noted above, & [1800].[12]

In the latter he is noted as Sr, with his son Richard Jr on the next line.

Children of Richard [2] & ?

+	12	i.	Richard Jr	b c1760
+	13	ii.	Robert	b 1794 d 187x

3. Jane Welborn [2] (Edward [1]), b ? d 1823? m to Stan

---

[11] Will footnote 1. It should be emphasized that the order here is the Will order– there is some evidence that the true order is different. See Table Five & discussion.

[12]   M recs, NCDAH 01 247.

U. S. Census Surry Co NC

1790 Richard Wilbourn household, Roll 7, p522, col 3 line 4

1800 Richard Wilborn household. Roll32, p698, line 13. The enroller either mixed up the Sr-Jr, or the handwriting is questionable as the age class noted for each Jr <1755 & Sr 1756-1774.

Loftus Sept 25th 1821. She is not mentioned in her brother John's 1819 Will. The 1823 Estate Surry Co NC may be hers. [13]

4. John Welborn [2] (Edward [1]), b c1754, d 1819, m Mary Hampton in 1783. His Will mentions wife Mary; brothers Richard, Edward, Zachary, Thomas & Lewis; Robert, son of Richard; & brother Thomas' children, unnamed; Sisters Temperance Marshall, Susannah L. Jones, & Lida (= Lydia?) Slaughter. The entry for Lewis requires some interpretation. [14]

No issue.

5. Thomas Welborn [2] (Edward [1]), b c1760 m ? d 1816 Thomas' only records found are in KY. [15]

---

[13]   Ancestry. Com on-line database. Granville Co Marriage Bonds (1763-1869); facsimile of marriage bond document, image 5550 of 9945.
Camin, Betty J., Surry County North Carolina Estates Index. Published by author, 1991?. This item is in The North Carolina State Library, Raleigh.

[14]   Marriage Holcomb, Brent, Marriages of Granville Co p 350.
Will Orange Co NC, Will Book D, folio 553, author has facsimile copy.
The exact wording in the Will: " I give and bequeath unto Lewis Wilborn Daniel, Betsy, and there two children Daniel and Nat. to him and his heirs etc etc" The interpretation here requires some additional information. Lewis is clearly a brother: the punctuation after 'Lewis' does not make clear what relations Daniel & Betsey are. This puzzle will be revisited under Lewis #8.

[15]   Heinemann, Chas B., First Census of Kentucky. G. Brumbaugh reprints; GPC 1993. (Original 1940).
Register, Kentucky Historical Society, GPC 1984, p156; 100A Madison Co, near brother Zachary.

U. S. Census

Children of Thomas [2] & ?

| + | 14 | i. | Robert | b c1775. |
| + | 15 | ii. | Edward | b c1790. |

6. Zachariah Welborn [2] (Edward [1]), b c1758 d? m Jemima White 1781. As what must have been the same Jemima White m Phillip White in 1783 some research must be done to attempt an explanation. [16]
Also in 1781 Zach served in the NC Continental Line listed in Pierces's Register. Zach's records are in Granville Co thence to Madison Co KY, with none found after [1810]. Both the State

---

1810 Cumberland Co KY, Thomas Wilbourn household. Roll 9, p706(749), lines 12-14. Age <1766, next to sons Robert & Edward..
N B Ancestry.com carries an entry for 1830 Hancock Co KY, Thomas Welborn household. Roll 37, p103, line 6th from bottom. Examination of the facsimile with magnification– the handwriting is faint– reveals the surname is actually Willis.
    1816 d is inferred from Cumberland Co Will Index, vol II, Book B, 1815-1840, Will filed 15 Feb.

[16] The records on Ancestry.com present a puzzle: a search for Jemima White with a d o b of c1760 produces a list of nine records involving Zach, Philip White & Jemima. First a Ledger, obviously typed, & with registrar numbers: viz
1781 White, Jemima   Zachariah Wilburn   6455.
Four (or more) records duplicated show on the same page
1783 White, Jemima   Philip White   6463.
Further under Jemima we find a handwritten version of the Ledger entry reading
1781 Wilburn Zachariah   Jemima White   Zach Wilburn
1773! White Philip   Jemima White   Philip White
(The third column here designates the Bondsman.)
The final entry is a facsimile of the legal document obligating Philip for a marriage bond payment to marry Jemima White. In this document the date is clearly 1783. Image 9361 of 9945.

Census & the [1810] list a son or sons, but no records have been found in KY that might possibly be his issue. [17]

7. Lewis Welborn [2] **(Edward** [1]**)**, b c1764 d >1840 m ?
Edward's son Lewis must be distinguished from others of the name, including a Generation 3 Lewis. There were Lewises in Johnston & Wilkes Cos that were not of Edward. The former of unknown origin, & the latter of Family F (next Section). Lewis [2] 's wife is not known, & Daniel is an uncertain son– he does not parse.

The children of Lewis [2] & ? [18]

+	16	i.	Richard	b c1805
+	17	ii.	James	b c1805
+	18	iii.	Lewis Jr	b 1802
		iv.	*Daniel*	b 1780-1800. This son is provisional depending on the interpretation of John2's Will.

---

[17]   1786 State census record, Nap of Reeds District, Granville Co (Register A. K.) with 1/2/3 dist., p 144; Madison Co KY; [1810] 1800 tax list in Madison Co KY, Oct 1st. Clift, G. Glen, "The Second Census of Kentucky, 1800". GPC various reprints 1966 - 2005. Original Frankfort KY, 1954.
U. S. Census
1810 Madison Co KY, Zachariah Wilburn household. Roll 7, p289, line 7. Age <1766,1 son <10, but 2 f >45.
Pierce's Register Register of the Certificates Issued by John Pierce, Esquire, Paymaster General and Commissioner of Army Accounts for the United States, to Officers and Soldiers of the Continental Army Under Act of July 4, 1783. U. S. Army War Department, 1915. Reprint 2012 Genealogical.com (GPC).

[18]   U. S. Census
1800 Wilkes Co NC, Lewis Willborn household. Roll 33, p69, line 2.
1830 Claiborne Co TN, Lewis Sr Wilbourn household. Roll 180, p108, Family group lines 3rd-6th from bottom. Age group 50-60. Next to Lewis Jr.

8. Edward [2] **(Edward** [1]**),**   b c1765   d 181x?   m Sarah Benham 1803 in Knox Co KY.

Edward Jr's records are difficult to distinguish from his father's. If the estimated d o b is approximately correct, he would not have achieved his majority until c1780. All records before 1782 can reasonable be assumed to be Edward Sr. If the SC & GA land records are Edward Sr's, then a 1784 land grant, as well as an 1785 Surry Co tax can be assigned to Jr at about age 19. His census, however, and a tax record are from Knox Co KY. [19]

Children of Edward 2 & Sarah

+   19   i.   William   b 1802.

Generation 3

12. Richard [3] **(Richard** [2]**, Edward** [1] **)** b c1760   d 1848   m Susannah Roberts 1791. Census [1800, thru 1840] all in Surry Co NC. He obtained land in 1801 along Camp Creek on the Surry-

---

[19]   1784 Land Grant, 50A north side of Yadkin River, Deed Book C, p169. Linn, Jo White, Surry County, North Carolina Wills 1771-1827. Genealogical Publishing Co., Baltimore, 1992

1786 census; distribution 1/3/3. This census can be read two ways: however, if Edward E1 had gone to Wilkes Co GA then the males must have been four of the sons. Register, Alvaretta, K., State Census of North Carolina. 2nd ed. revised, GPC 1971, p144.

1793 land, 50A metes & bounds only– MARS 12.14.113.2261.

1800 tax, Knox Co KY. Registers of the Kentucky Historical Society. GPC 1983, p107.

U. S. Census 1810 Knox Co KY, Edward Wilbourn household. Roll 7, p86(664), line 16.

1812, War of. Capt in 14th KY Militia. fold3 image #309574281. In the same unit was William Wilburn, pvt, designated below as his son.

Wilkes border. His Will & Estate are in Surry Co. [20]

13. Robert [3] (Richard [2], Edward [1])   b 1794 !   d 187x   m
Eliz. ?
Robert's records, as are his brother's are all in Surry Co. Census
[1830 thru 1870, missing 1850]. The [1860] carries a d o b of 1795:
[1870], age b 1797, is with a Sally W- age 41 b NC (she is likely a
daughter as the [1840] includes two females b 1830-1840.)
He must have had land, but only a land entry record is in the
DataBase. [21]

14. Robert [3] (Thomas [2], Edward [1])   b 1775   d ?
This Robert's records are all from census in KY & IL. The crucial
one is the [1810] in Cumberland Co KY which placed him next to his
father & brother Edward. The [1830, 1840, & 1850] are all from

---

[20]   MARS 12.14.113.2195. In 1803 he was a chain carrier
for a Wm Seagroves survey. NCGSJ May 88 vol 14, p85.
     U. S. Census Surry Co NC
1800 Richard Wilborn jr household. Roll 32, p698, line 3. Age class
>45; next to his father. The census listing is alphabetic.
1810 Richard Wilbourn household. Roll 43, p673, 3rd from bottom.
1820 Richard Wilbourn household. Roll 82, p666, line 2nd from bottom
1830 Richard Willbern household. Roll 125, p119, line 16. Age class
60-70.
1840 Richard Wilbourn household. Roll 116, p371, line 13. Age class
70-80.
     1848 Will, Surry Co, Book 4 #276, NC Wills & Probate
Records, 1665-1998. Facsimile print of index im 25/298 available
Ancestry.com on-line database. In Estate record im 421/2040 has
partial? list of heirs.

[21]   H. Steel enters 100A 1841, bordering Robert Wilburn. No
water course. Pruitt, A. B., Abstracts of Land Entries. Holdings Surry
County. 1784-1795. By author, 1987- 1992. This extensive series is
by County.

Sangamon Co IL. [22]

15. Edward [3] (Thomas [2], Edward [1]) b c1785   d ?
After the [1810] above, subsequent records are in KY & possibly
MO. [23]

16. Lewis Jr [3] (Lewis [2], Edward [1])   b 1802 d >1880 m
Eliz. ?   This Lewis moved often; census in TN, KY, & IN. His d o
b given therein as 1801, 1802, & 1808.[24]

---

[22]   U. S. Census
1810 Cumberland Co KY, Robert Wilbourn household. Roll 9, p174,
image 00183; next to Edward & Thomas, lines 12-14.
1830 Sangamon Co IL, Robert Wilbourn household. Roll 24, p152, line
11.
1840 Sangamon Co IL, Robert Wilbourn household. Roll 69, p24, 5th
b 1775 in NC; wife Eliz. b 1790 VA.
 from bottom.
1850 Sangamon Co IL, Robert Wilbourn household. Roll 127, p237B,
family 1540.

[23] U. S. Census
1820 Cumberland Co KY, Edward Wilbourn household. Roll 19, p140,
line 14. Age class 1775-1794, next to Gen 4 sons William & ? both b
1794-1804 .
1830 Jackson Co MO, Edward Wilbourn household. Roll 70, p306, 5th
from bottom. Age class 50-60.

[24]   U. S. Census
1830 Claiborne Co TN, Lewis Jr Wilbourn household. Roll 180, p108,
6th from bottom, image 417. Family group w/Lewis Sr.
1840 Carter Co KY, Lewis Wilburn household. Roll 107, p246, line 1.
1850 Carter Co KY, Lewis Wilbourn household. Roll 195, p264B,
family 213. Age b 1808TN. Eliz. 42TN
1860 Carter Co KY, Lewis Wilburn household. Roll 361, p175, Family
189. Age 1802NC, Eliz. 59TN.
1870 Crawford Co IN, Lewis Wilburn household. Roll 306, p 183,
family 148.

17. James ³ (Lewis ², Edward ¹)   b c1795   d ?

The only record found is the Family census in the Claiborne TN [1830] along with the Lewises, Sr & Jr, & brother Richard. Footnote ibid.

18. Richard ³ (Lewis ², Edward ¹)   b c 1795   d ?

As above. All three of Lewis ² sons parse in the [1800] Wilkes NC.

19. William ³ (Edward ², Edward ¹)   b c1802,   d ?

Three census, all in KY help comprise his Family E record. He is, doubtless, the William that served in the War of 1812 in The 15ᵗʰ KY Militia, his father's unit. footnote 19 above   ²⁵

Age 1801NC, Eliz. 69TN.
1880 Bullitt Co KY, Lewis Wilburn household. Roll 107, p246, line 1. Age 78 b NC.

²⁵   U. S. Census
1820 Cumberland Co KY William Wilbourn household. Roll 19, p140 (163), line 13. Next to his cousin Edward #15 1775-1794. Make sure yes Ed 2 b c1765.
1830 Russell Co KY, William Wilborn household. Roll 41, p123, line 18. Age class 1800-1810.
1840 Russell Co KY, William Wilbourn household. Roll 123, p32, line 20. Age class 1800-1810.

FAMILY F   ISAAC WELBORN Progenitor

Précis

This Family & the next, Family G, were in Generations 2 & 3 located in the same region of the Old Granville District– the watershed area of the Yadkin River where Surry, Stokes & Forsyth Counties abut. This circumstance makes separation of like-named individuals difficult, problems that are treated below.

Generation 1

Isaac according to a Findagrave record was b 1732 in MD & left a Stokes Co Estate in 1798. This Estate record lists in order; heirs William, Isaac, John, Samuel, James, & Daniel. (For the daughters see the Formal Genealogy below.)[1]

Isaac was a very early resident of The Granville District with a number of records 1755-1760, in what was then Rowan Co. When Surry Co was formed in 1770 & Wilkes in 1777, further records proved to be in those two Cos. As the Wilkes & Surry records for the sons also include some of Stokes Co , formed 1789, some effort was made to identify the Family Lands. Again, the presence of Isaac Jr

---

[1]   The Findagrave #68312432 material includes information from the Stokes Co Estate Papers. This author queried The Stokes Co Library & was graciously rewarded by a facsimile copy of the Record. A facing page reads " A List of the Heirs of Isaac Wellbourn decdy (sic). I have asu?fd them to Shew why the Lands Should (the rest untranslatable), /s/ March 1800". This strip of text is followed by a single page listing, clearly, the heirs. The Estate is also mentioned in Camin, Betty J., Surry County North Carolina Estates Index. Published by author, 1991?, p18. This item is in The North Carolina State Library, Raleigh.

complicates the separation of records as to father-&-son.[2]

In 1779 Isaac was the assignee of Mary Morris of 200A on Sweedons Fork of Greasey Creek. Ten years later Isaac deeded that land to son William of Stokes Co.[3] How do we read 'Greasey' ? The first guess would be as Grassy. On p5, Chapter One, this location was judged to be a Grassy Creek that lies close to the then Surry-Guilford line– today on the Surry-Stokes border. In some of the land records the Wachovia Line is mentioned, e g in May of 1789, Isaac acquired 200A on the Grasy (sic) Branch, Sibeden Fork along the Wachovia Line. The Carolina Gazetteer places the Wachovia Tract, 1755, in North-east Rowan Co, today's Forsyth Co.

For the Isaacs, Sr & Jr, land & tax records occur in both Wilkes & Surry Cos. Two deed transfers in 1785, Surry, could have been either– the location was 'In Surry & Stokes Counties below the mouth of the Little Yadkin on Big Yadkin.' This location today is where Surry-Stokes & Forsyth Cos abut, & is almost surely the

---

[2] 1755 NC Early Census Ancestry On-line database Isaac Wilbourn, Rowan Co NC (original Jackson R.V. North Carolina Census, 1790-1890). Maybe the same as 1759 Rowan Co Tax List-Linn, Jo White, Abstracts of Wills & Estate Records of Rowan County, 1753-1805 and Tax Lists 1759 & 1778. By author, Salisbury, 1980. 1758 Isaac grantee from J. Fullerlane (no A or watercourse given) Book 4, folio 327, Index to Real Estate Conveyances, 1753-1921, Reel 254 Rowan Co Deed Records. In 1797 Isaac of Surry Co together with his wife Rebekah deeded this land to James Garrison of Rowan; Kluttz, James W., Abstracts of Deed Books Rowan County, North Carolina, Deed Books 15-19 , 1797-1807; 769, p 561.
1760 Isaac Welbourn grantee 158A Rowan Co, deed book 4 pp327-9 found on Index of Real Estate Conveyances 1753-1921, Reel #254, Rowan Co.
1793 Isaac Wilborn, tax list Wooton District Wilkes Co, Ancestry.com on-line database. Original Jackson R. V. Early NC Census 1790-1890.

[3] MARSid #12.14.107.2544. 1789 Rowan Co Bk 18 #1651, p 62 fide Kluttz series, p820.

Grassy Creek property. A 1793 tax list places an Isaac in the Wootten District of Wilkes Co.[4]
Thus, the Family F of Isaac was centered on a region that, historically, provides records in four Counties; Rowan, Wilkes, Surry, & Stokes (Forsyth Co was created in 1849, from Stokes). In 1785 Isaac, either Sr or Jr, acquired land in Surry Co in the region described above. One record was a transfer in 1795 of 640A ! from Arther Scott of Stokes Co to Edward Lovell, James Thompson, & Isaac Welburn for 1000 pounds below mouth of little Yadkin on Big Yadkin.[5]

Generation 2

The order of heirs listed on the Estate record is Elizabeth (Swaim), Ann (Bean), William, Isaac, John, Rebecka (Killion), Samuel, Mary, James, & Daniel. Judging from the dates established from the records (below), this was the birth order. In [1790], Isaac Sr had distribution 4/2/5, & Isaac Jr 1/1/1. Parsing the Sr census results in the two b 1774-1790 to be James & Daniel; & the four Isaac Sr, William, John & Samuel; consistent with the order of the heirs. The individual d o bs are given below & agree with the parsing.
William's first record appears to be in 1780 when he acquired 100A on North side of the Yadkin River. His father granted him land along

---

[4] Powell, William S., The Carolina Gazetteer, UNC Press, 1968. Delorme Atlas, p16, panel C-2. See also Table Three.
1793 tax footnote 2 previous. No information was found as to the location of the Wootten District.

[5] Absher, Mrs W.O., Surry County, North Carolina deed abstracts. Books D,E, & F, 1779-1797. Southern Historical Press, Easley SC, 1985. Book F #019, p235,
This very large tract must have been purchased by a Combine- £ 1000 was also a very large sum for the times.
Ibid Book D, p109. Deed transfer J. Carson to Isaac, 2A! Forbis Creek on 18/6/1795. On p 126 this land was sold by Isaac Sr to E. Lovell, 5/9/1796, with William Welborn a witness. Presumably the same Isaac.

Greasey (Grassy) Crk in 1789. He also /s/ a bill, 1794, to establish a town in Stokes Co. His final record in the DataBase is [1800] Stokes Co.[6] As far as can be determined, John left only that single record. The location, Stokes Co, points to the Family, with his brother William nearby.[7]

Samuel, on the other hand, left census [1810 thru 1840] all in Wilkes Co. These, however, seem to be the only records available– no land/deeds were found: He might be confused with Samuel C. of Family C.[8]

James, F2, a Blacksmith by trade, left many records & many children– see the Formal Genealogy below. He resided in Wilkes Co his entire life; census enrolling him [1820 thru 1860]. It is important to distinguish him from the C2 James as both resided in Wilkes Co.

---

[6]   1780 MARS 12.14.124.279 & Linn, Jo White, Surry County, North Carolina Wills 1771-1827. Genealogical Publishing Co., Baltimore, 1992. Annotated genealogical abstracts, p12.
1789 MARS 12.14.124.342.
1794. MARS search GASR 66.8.73.17.5.
U.S. census
1800 Stokes Co NC, William Wilborn household. Roll 32, p576, line 1; Age class 1755-1774.

[7] U.S. census
1800 Stokes Co NC, John Wilborn household. Roll 32, p613, line 10.
Age class 1755-1774.

[8]   U. S. Census, Wilkes Co NC
1810 Samuel Wellborn household. Roll 43, p 273(860) line 16.
1820 Samuel Willborn household. Roll 83, p376, 3rd line from bottom.
1830 Samuel Willborn household. Roll 125, p373, line 12. Age class 1770-1780.
1840 Samuel Wellborn household. Roll 373, p108, 3rd line from bottom. Age class 1770-1780, alone.

See Chapter Two, Part Three, p37. [9]

Daniel, F2 the youngest son of Isaac lived only about 50 years– his d o b is uncertain. Census [1820 1830]. There is an 1849 Estate File for Daniel that includes Family history that affects his descendants. In Aug of 1847 two of his daughters, Catherine & Martha, filed suit against the two of sons, Daniel H. & Francis M(ontgomery). The second-born son Thomas S. is not mentioned in the suit. The squabble was over the details of Daniel's death-bed wishes, & ultimately the division of his land. In the Court's May of 1849 apportionment, six names appear (aside from Thomas S. & Daniel H.): Elvira, Sarah Smith, Nancy, James W., Isaac deceased w/heirs Elizabeth & Rebecca, & James James (sic).

Speculation here suggest the females are Daniel's daughters; & that James W. & Isaac are sons. Testing this speculation with parsing of the [1820 & 1830] does admit the two sons if b 1804-1810. The daughters would fit the parse if the three were b also 1804-1810. The last name-James James (sic)- is a complete mystery.

In the Formal Genealogy, the above sons & daughters are listed as Daniel's descendants. [10]

---

[9]   U. S. Census, Wilkes Co NC

1820 James Wellborn household. Roll 83, p506, 4th line from bottom. The occupation & economic summary on p549.

1830 James Willbern household. Roll 125, p372, line 11. Age class 1770-1780.

1840 James Wellborn household. Roll 373, p5, line 19. Age class 1770-1780.

1850 James Willborn household. Roll 649, p363, righthand line 24. The page is folded & cannot be completely read. b 1778 Rowan Co, Rebecca b1790 Wilkes.

1860 James Willborn household. Roll 918, p109, family 122. Rebecca 66, James 26, Rebecca 20, Lewis 19. Next to son Daniel, Family 123.

[10]   U. S. Census, Wilkes Co NC

1820 Daniel Willborn household. Roll 83, p498, line 1. Age class 1775-1794.

1830 Daniel Wellborn household. Roll 125, p393, line 23. Age class

Generation 3

The two eldest sons William & Isaac both had issue specified by [1800]. Of these, all had d o bs from 1784-1800 & no candidates appear in the record. Third son John's [1800] listed only females b1790-1800. Samuel's record contains two possibly three sons b 1800-1810 & one 1810-1820, & four daughters 1804-1810--see below.

James, the Blacksmith, however can be credited with at least seven sons & a daughter all by census– a circumstance of a long life that lasted into the [1850 & 1860].

Daniel, the youngest son, also had issue. Nearly all can be identified either thu census or judicious parsing.

A special account must be given here– for William Welborn b Guilford Co in 1809, d 1879; and was m three times. He appears in the Family bible with the vital and marriage data.[11] The three m mentioned, to Esther Charles in Feb of 1834; Mary Charles in Oct, 1839; & to Christine Raper in May of 1858 (sic) are all documented. Christina was b in July of 1838 & as a widow lived until 1929. She was one of four daughters of Davis Raper of the Deep River District

---

1780-1790.
North Carolina Estate Files, 1663-1979, FamilySearch database w/images: Wilkes Co NCDAH; FHL mfilm 2,318,019.

[11]   Genealogical data from bibles in the possession of the North Carolina Historical Commission. Transcribed by The North Carolina DAR. Family History Library Catalog , FHL US/CAN Film 18067, item 3, p 46. At the time the bible was transcribed, it was in the possession of John W. Welborn of Kernersville, NC.
North Carolina Marriage Bonds, 1741-1868. Esther Charles to William Welborn, Feb 1, 1834 & Mary Charles to William Welborn, Oct 7, 1839, 03 473, im 501/652 Guilford Co m bonds; Christina Raper to William Welborn, May 13, 1862, Ancestry on-line database im 589 of 2997. We note that the bondsman for Wm & Esther was David M. Welborn.

of Stokes, later Forsyth Co. She is buried in the Abbotts Creek
Baptist Cemetery in present Davidson Co.[12]

From these records we know that William was b Guilford Co
& married there. But there are no Wm W-. census in Guilford of
correct age 1820 - 1840. So- the puzzle is where was William &
wives? Consideration of the locations of the records above (Stokes,
Forsyth, & Abbotts Creek) point to the region where the three
Counties abut today, (north of Kernersville).[13]   Thus, this
circumstance applies to a William Welborn with census [1840 thru
1870] in Stokes & Forsyth Cos. [14] This information leads to

---

[12]   Will of Davis Raper, Ancestry on-line database, im 61 of
414 from NCDAH C.R. 038 801 92, Forsyth Co. The four Christina
E.; Herzeah L., Margaret E., & Sarah L.
     U. S. census
1880 Forsyth Co NC, Cristin(a) Welborn household. Roll 963, p412B,
family 141. Age 41NC w/ two young sons.
NC Death Index 1908-2004, Ancestry on-line databse, age 91,
Davidson Co. Findagrave #16288018, burial information w/no photo.

[13]   DeLorme Atlas, p17, panel C5. Note location of Family
bible, footnote 12.

[14]   U. S. census
1840 Stokes Co NC, Deep River, William Wilbourn household. Roll
154, p372, line 8. age class 5, 1810-1820. (There is another male in the
same age class, probably a brother.)
1850 Forysth Co NC, William Wilborne household. Roll 630, p228A,
family 423. age 37NC, with issue ages 9,7, &4; & Christina
Montgomery 24NC. Note: his marriage to Christina Raper was in
1862.
1860 Forsyth Co NC, Deep River, William Wilborn household. Roll
897, p332, family722. Age 51NC. family includes Christina
Montgomery 28 ! His wife Christina Raper Welborn was b 1838 & the
marriage record stipulates 1862. All this opens a puzzle as to just what
was his marital status & why is the information on Christina– if all the
same person– so contradictory.
1870 Fosyth Co NC, Abbotts Creek. Roll 1137, p301A, family 67.
Christina 30 & infant son.

examining Family F for the parents of William.

Only two of the Generation 2 Welborns had sons in the 1800-1810 (1809) time frame, Daniel & Samuel. To chose & assign we note that the census indicates that William had records starting, and not before, 1840. A parsing of Samuel has records of a son b 1800-1810 in [1810, 1820, 1830] & Daniel does in [1820 & 1830]. The [1810] for Daniel is missing! So, at this point we must leave the precise assignment of William's parentage open– either Samuel or Daniel are candidates.

William & first wife Esther's bondsman was a David M. Welborn. The Database includes a David M. Welborn b 1811/1812, a resident of Lafayette Co MO in [1850, 1870, 1880] Was he a sibling or cousin. He cannot be of Daniel B2– his age class is full, but he does fit into Samuel's. The parsing does strongly suggest that both William & David M. are of Samuel F2.

In attempting a parse of Family F, Gen 2 there is a single record, a census, of a Sydney Welborn from Wilkes Co. b 1810-1820 age class. With but a single record– and from Wilkes Co– it may never be possible to place him.[15]

---

footnote # above. 1880 Forsyth Co NC, Cristin(a) Welborn household. Roll 963, p412B, family 141. A widow age 41NC.

[15]   U. S. census Lafayette Co MO
1850 David M. Wilborn household. Roll 403, p233B, family 1254. Age 38NC, wife Catherine, sons Moses, Wm, Jacob, daus Eliz. Mary R.
1870 David M. Wilborn household. Roll 786, p253A, family 404. Age 58, widower, w/Moses, Wm, & John.
1880 David M. Welborn household. Roll 698, p321D, family 232. Age 69NC, parents b NC.
    U. S. census
1840 Wilkes Co NC, Becknels Dist., Sydney Welborn household. Roll 373, p70 (241), line 10. Issue.

FORMAL GENEALOGY

Generation 1
1. Isaac Welborn[1], b 1732 d 1798 m Rebecca ?

A summary of Isaac's records is given above: Rebecca's maiden name is not known, but she was enrolled [1800] Stokes Co as a widow, b<1756.

Children of Isaac[1] & Rebecca ? [16]

+	2	i	William	b c1760
+	3	ii.	Isaac	b c1760
+	4	iii.	John	b c1760
+	5	iv.	Samuel	b 1773
+	6	v.	James	b 1778
+	7	vi.	Daniel	b c1783
	8	vii.	Elizabeth	m John Swaim
	9	viii.	Ann	m Nicholas Bean
	10	ix.	Rebecca	m John Killion
	11	x.	Mary	unmarried ?

Generation 2
2.   William[2] (Isaac[1])   b c1760 d<1810 m Hessibee ?

This, the eldest son lived in Wilkes & Stokes Co, possibly on the same land. Two records totaling 500A & an important document specifying his wife & father are to his credit. The latter, a facsimile that has been translated by this author, is an indenture, a contract, between William & Josiah Lamb for a tract in Randolph Co. It reads in part: "This indenture made this Eighteenth day of March in The year of our Lord one thousand seven hundred & eighty five between

---

[16]   U. S. Census
1800 Stokes Co NC, Rebeckah Wilborne houshold. Roll 32, p575, last line. b <1756. Two sons 1774-1784 (James & Daniel) & three daughters. Son William is the next family.
The order is that of the Estate listing, which based on the material in this Genealogy seems to be born out.

William Welborn of Wilkes County & State of North Carolina & Hessissibee (sic) his wife & for in {??} of the sum of Thirty Pounds Specie to them in hand paid by the said Josiah Lamb ...... a certain tract or parcel of land which fell to the aforesaid William Welborn by heirship from Isaac deceased who purchased the same from the aforesaid William Welborn ...... ".
His only census is [1800] with issue indicated. An effort to identify these has been unsuccessful. [17]

3.   **Isaac^2 (Isaac^1)**   b c1760   m Elvira Tomlinson   d?
Records are [1790] & [1800] Surry Co.   Owing to the Sr-Jr relationship, other records may apply to either. There are two land transfers in Surry Co, 1795 & 1796. As his father seemed to be in Stokes Co, these were probably of Isaac Jr. In 1800, Isaac of Surry Co was grantor of 200A Greasey (sic) Branch to William Wilborn of Stokes Co. These are certainly brothers– the two eldest sons. Note the Counties specified & the discussion of the Families' location given above. [18]

---

[17]   Facsimile from Randolph County Deed Book 2, folio 124. The signatures-marks are as written Wm Welborn Jur & He(ss)i(ss)ibee Welborn. The (ss)= the thong– why double is a mystery. 1780 land. 100A n side of Yadkin, MARS 12.14.124.279 Warrant 400A same location MARS 12.14. 24.342. William a grantee from Isaac of Surry Co.
1794 petition to establish a town Stokes Co GASR MARS 66.8.73.17.5
        U. S. Census
1800 Stokes Co NC, William Wilborn household. Roll 32, p576, line 1. Age class 1755-1774. Two males b 1790-1800 & three females also 1790-1800.
No [1810] can be found & parsing with available material does not suggest any candidates.

[18]   1795, Isaac grantee w/a combine of grantees, 640A Surry & Stokes Cos below the mouth of the Little, Surry & Stokes.- Absher, Mrs W.O., Surry County, North Carolina deed abstracts. Books D,E, & F, 1779-1797. Southern Historical Press, Easley SC, 1985, Bk F#109,

From the [1790 & 1800] Isaac & his wife had issue: in the former a single son & in the latter three sons b1790-1800 & two daughters 1790-1800 & 1784-1790; & apparently a widower. Again parsing with available records does not suggest who this issue might be.

4.   John[2] (Isaac[1])   b 1765   d ?
The only sure reference to this John is the [1800] Stokes Co. (See Chapter One, Part One.) In this census, only daughters are listed, two <10. [19]

5.   Samuel[2] (Isaac[1])   b 1773   d 184x   m ?
Samuel was located in Wilkes Co his entire life; enrolled in all [1810 thru 1840]. No land/deed records were found. From the census, the couple had issue, but their identification depends upon the material above on William & David M. Parsing produces a fit [1810], two males & females 1800-1810: [1820] one male 1810-1820; one 1804-1810; & four females 1804-1820. [20]

---

p235.
1795 Isaac grantee of 2A Forbis Creek from J. Carson: in 1796 Isaac transferred this small plot to E. Lovell. Surry Co, Ibid.
1800 Kluttz, James W., Abstracts of Deed Books Rowan County, North Carolina. Abstracts of Deed Books 15-19, 1797-1807, pub Cary NC, 1997, Book 18, p62.
M Isaac & Elvira Tomlinson, from County Court Records, Wilkes Co–Ancestry.com on-line database. No date.

[19]   U.S. census
1800 Stokes Co NC, John Wilborn residence. Roll 32, p613, line10. Age class 1755-1774.

[20]   There is a puzzling record for a Samuel Wellbourn serving in the Sixteenth Company, Haywood Co Regiment in 1812. The Co in far western NC. If Samuel[2], he served far from home. Ancestry.com, North Carolina Compiled Census & Census Substitutes Index, 1790-1890 Original from Jackson, R. V.
U. S. Census, Wilkes Co NC

Sons of Samuel[2] & ?

12	i.	*Isaac*	*b 1800-1810*
13	ii.	William	b 1809
14	iii.	David M.	b 1812

6.   James[2] (Isaac[1]) b 1778,   d 1861,   m Rebecca ? b 1790.

James was a Blacksmith by trade, specified by the [1820]. As with three of his brothers, all records are from Wilkes Co. Census [1820 thru 1860]. The latter of these give his wife as Rebecca b1790 in Wilkes Co. His Will was filed in April of 1861: heirs son James, granddaughter Caroline Russel; w/executor son Daniel. Generation 3 for James & Rebecca is from census & parsing.

The children of James[2] & Rebecca [21]

1810 Samuel Wellborn household. Roll 43, p273(860), line 16.
1820 Samuel Wellborn household. Roll 83, p376, 3rd line from bottom.
1830 Samuel Willborn household. Roll 125, p373, line 121; image 1 Wilkesboro
        This page is not searchable on Ancestry.com presumably because the page is split- top Wilkes Co, bottom Wilkesboro. Age class 50-60; wife 40-50.
1840 Samuel Wellborn household. Roll 373, p108, 3rd from bottom. Age class 60-70, alone.
1830 Isaac Wellborn household. Roll 125, p394, line 1. b 1800-1810, Issue.
1860 Forsyth Co NC, William Wilborn household. Roll 897, p332, family 722, b 1809.

[21]   Confusing dates are given for James & daughter Rebecca. The problem arises principally owing to the infamous folded page in the [1850]– see footnote 9. The names are partly obscured, but are reasonably read as James 22 & Rebecca 15. Both are next to, but not necessarily in the same Family as, ?ames 72 b Rowan & ?becah 60 b Wilkes. Possibly, the old folks confused the ages of the younger pair. In any case, the [1860] for James Sr specified James as 26, & Rebecca as 20. The third child is Lewis 19. In any case the parsing for James &

+	15	i.	Daniel	b 1817/1818
+	16	v.	Lewis J.	b 1825
+	17	iii.	James	b 1828
+	18	iv.	Rebecca	b 1835/1840

7.   Daniel^2 (Isaac^1)   b c1783   d 1834   m Sarah Douglas 1803 Daniel's Will lists only heirs Daniel H, Francis Montgomery, and Susan Senanthey(sic) underage with Daniel Herman Wellborn executor. See the discussion of his Estate file, p 157 above.

Children of Daniel^2 & Sarah [22]

+	19	i.	Daniel H.	b 1812
+	20	ii.	Thomas S.	b 1814
+	21	ii.	F. Montgomery	b 1817

Rebecca's children fits perfectly.

1861 Will. Turner, Grace & Miles S. Philbeck, comps, Wilkes County North Carolina Will Abstracts, 1777-1910. By authors, Wilson Co., NC, 1988, #758. Mentioned in the Will: Wife Rebecca, son James, & executor Daniel.

[22]   Marriage NCDAH 03 336, avaiable Ancestry.com. Wm Welborn, bond.

U. S. Census Wilkes Co NC

1820   Daniel Willborn household. Roll 83, p498, line 1. Age class 1775-1794, three sons 1810-1820, 2 1804-1810; two daughters 1810-1820, one 1804- 1810.

1830   Daniel Wellborn household. Roll 125, p393, line 23. Two sons, 1825-1830, 1800-1810; daughters 1825-1830, two 1820-1825. Will March 2 1834. Turner, Grace & Miles S. Philbeck, comps, Wilkes County North Carolina Will Abstracts, 1777-1910. By authors, Wilson Co., NC, 1988. #756. From Book 4, folio 178.

1870 Washington Co TN, Sarah Wellborn household. Roll 1568, p235B, family 13. Sarah 81, Catherine 45, Martha E. 42. Next to son Thomas S.

1880 Washington Co TN, Thomas Wellborn household. Roll 1284, p515B, family 15. Thos 67, Mary A 66; Catherine 55, Martha 52; the sisters unmarried.

22	iii.	Susan S.	b c1825	
23	iv.	Catherine	b 1825	Unmarried
24	v.	Martha E.	b 1828	Unmarried
25	*vi.*	*Elvira*	*b ?*	
26	*vii.*	*Nancy*	*b ?*	
27	*viii.*	*James W.*	*b ?*	
28	*ix.*	*Isaac*	*b ? d as of 1849*	

Generation 3

12. Isaac³ (Samuel², Isaac¹)   the only record is [1830].[23]

13. William³ (Samuel², Isaac¹)

14. David M. ³ (Samuel², Isaac¹)   See discussion above: footnotes 15 & 16.

15. Daniel³ (James², Isaac¹)   b 1817   m Susanna Deal in 1836   d 1885 leaving a Will. Census all Wilkes Co [1840, 1850, 1860, 1880].[24]

---

[23]   U. S. census
1830 Wilkes Co NC, Isaac Wellborn houshold. Roll 125, p384, line 1. age class 20-30. Issue. This Isaac may belong to Family C- he does parse with Samuel.

[24]   M record Wilkes Co NC 11/2/1836 Daniel Welborn to Susanna Deal. County Court Records, FHL #0546475 & 0546481.
            U.S. census Wilkes Co NC
1840 Daniel Welborn household. Roll 373, p 58. Line 18. Next to father James.
1850 Daniel Willborn household. Roll 649, p363, line 17. Bb 1817 Wilkes, Susanna b 1815 Lincoln Co. Next to father James.
1860 Daniel Willborn household. Roll 918, p109, family 123.
1880 Daniel Willborn household. Roll 987, p126A, ED214, family47. Susannah 65, all parents b NC.

16. Lewis J. [3] **(James** [2] **, Isaac** [1] **)**   b 5/1824   m Susan Miranda Watson in 1848   d 4/1909.
Lewis' middle name according to Findagrave was Johnson. [25]

17. James [3] **(James** [2] **, Isaac** [1] **)**   b 1828?   m Martha ?
d >1900
Remained in his father's household thru 1860. Census in [1880 & 1900]. [26]

18. Rebecca [3] **(James** [2] **, Isaac** [1] **)**   b 1840   d ?
The only records found for this daughter were the [1850 & 1860]. The d o b confusion is explained above, footnote 21, which specifies 1835 & [1860] b 1840, probably more reliable as she was still in her

---

Will Daniel Welbourn, Wilkes Co WillBook 6, folio 261. Turner, Grace & Miles S. Philbeck, comps, Wilkes County North Carolina Will Abstracts, 1777-1910. By authors, Wilson Co., NC, 1988.

[25] M 16/12/1848 Wilkes Co NC. NCDAH marriage bonds #02 260. Lewis J. Wellborn & Susan Miranda Watson.
Findagrave # 75098290, burial Stony Fork Baptist Cemetery, Watauga Co, good original stone.
U. S. Census
1850 Wilkes Co NC, Lewis J Wellborn household. Roll 649, p368, family 1773. Age 25, Susan 21.
1870 Watauga Co NC, Lewis Welborn household.roll 1164, p842B, family 56. Age 45, Susan 40. Issue five sons, three daughters.
1880 Watauga Co NC, Daniel Willborn household. Lewis J. Father age 76. Mary C., sister 85. Roll 1223, p80, ED0131, family 134.

[26] Census footnote 21, for James F2.
U.S. census Wilkes Co NC
1880 James Wellborn household. Roll 987, p126, ED 214, family 45. James 52, Martha 38, issue.
1900 James Wellborn household. Roll 1224, p128. ED 0143, family 231. James 73, Martha 55. W/two sons.

father's household.[27]

19. Daniel H.[3] (Daniel[2], Isaac[1])   b 1812   m Sarah Brown d 1884.

Tracing Daniel H. thru time is a bit confused. That he was a son of Daniel[2] is given by the latter's Will. Footnote 22. There is a [1850] in Schuyler Co MO, with a definite m i of H, giving age 38 with Sarah same age. Two sons, Francis & Newton ages 9 & 5 were b TN, but no [1840] TN lists a Daniel. In [1870] this Daniel was in Van Buren Co IA, w/Sarah, both age 58. A Findagrave has him buried in that County, with vital data b Jan 29 1812 d Aug 14 1884, with middle name of Harmon. These seem reasonable, but the record indicates a birth in Guilford Co NC & as the memorial stone is very modern this attribution is probably false. There is a record of a Daniel Welborn m Sarah Coffin Guilford Co in 1838 and whose Findagrave record has him buried in Guilford Co with d o b of Oct 30, 1812. That perhaps has led to the misplaced birth location. The Daniel H of MO & IA is the son of Daniel F2. [28]

---

[27]   U.S. census Wilkes Co NC
1860 James Wellborn household. Roll 918, p 109, family 122; same as footnote 21.

[28] U. S census
1850 Schuyler Co MO, Daniel H Welborn household. Roll 419, p105A, family 419. Both Daniel & Sarah b NC, age 38.
1870 Van Buren Co IA, Daniel H Wellborn household. Roll421, p348A, family 283. David & Sarah b 58.
1880 Van Buren Co IA, R. L. Wilbern household. Roll 367, p525D, family 76. Daniel H. 71 & Sarah 72 as father & mother included. Daniel's father b VA, mother NC, which raises some questions as Daniel F2 b VA?
     Marriage Sarah Brown from Findagrave #99666228; no record has been found.
     Findagrave for the Guilford Daniel is #49031677, with original stone.

20.   Thomas S .[3] **(Daniel**[2]**, Isaac**[1]**)**   b 12/1813   m Mary A. Templeton   d 1/1900.
Thomas lived in Wilkes Co until the mid-1860s, moving to Washington Co TN where he d in 1900. A Findagrave record gives his vital data as b 12/3/1813 & d 1/20/1900; & his middle name as Shepard. A son J. R. (James R.) was named as executor of the estate.[29]

21.   F. Mongomery[3] **(Daniel**[2]**, Isaac**[1]**)**   b 1817 m Nancy ? d?
The only record found, other than as an heir of Daniel, is the [1860]. The wife is Nancy & the family large. He is not found in any listing of Confederate soldiers.[30]

---

[29]   U. S. Census
1840 Wilkes Co NC, Kilbys District, Thomas Wellborn household. Roll 373, p55, line 6th from bottom. Age 20-30 wife   & a 80-90 female.
1850 Wilkes Co NC, Thomas Wellborn household. Roll 649, p280B, family 831. Wife Mary 34 b Iredell {Ancestry.com erroneous gives her birth as in Ireland.}. Issue.
1860 Wilkes Co NC, Thomas Willborn household. Roll 918, p123, family 335. Thomas bSurry, Mary A b Iredell.
1870 Washington Co TN, Thomas Willborn household. Roll 1568, p255B, families 12 & 13. Sarah (mother) 81 with his sisters Catherine & Martha next door.

1880 Washington Co TN, Thomas Wellborn household. Roll 1284, p515B, family 15. Thos 67, Mary A 66; the sisters unmarried.
Findagrave #88585202, burial in Oak Hill Cemetery, Johnson City TN. Original stone.
Washington Co State of Tennessee Court, April 2nd 1900. TN Wills & Probate, 1779-2009, Probate records 1778-1950, p213. Ancestry.com on-line database.

[30] U. S. Census
1860 Wilkes Co NC, Montgomery Wilborn household. Roll 918, p122, family 332. Age 43, Nancy 40.; six sons, three daughters.

FAMILY G   JOHN WELBORN Progenitor

Précis

This Family was a comparatively latecomer to the Old Granville District; the earliest record the [1810] in Wilkes Co. John was b c1760, apparently in VA.[1] Owing to his relatively late birth, he is placed in Generation 2 (along with the John of Family D). He is a John who must be distinguished from the others– fortunately in this Family such can be done with considerable confidence (see Chapter Two, Part One). The naming of the children & grandchildren is as distinctive as is found throughout the Families. Along with the share of English royalty (John, Henry, & James), the Family includes an Abel, Allen, Marbury, & Joel.

The Family was located in Wilkes Co thru Generations 3 & 4 with little evidence of emigration to other States. There is a lack of land & deed records in The DataBase. The reference material consulted, Appendix One; as well as the MARS, contained no citations to Family G members.

Generation 3

Johns & Lucy Ann's children come with excellent records and the parsing of their [1810] & [1820] results in all of the sons accounted for. The only daughter is tentatively identified. The eldest two sons, Henry b1793 & Marbury b1796 both born in VA, giving credence to

---

[1]   John's full name, origin & marriage are from FamilyTree. One source gives his name as John J. S. Wilborn; another specifying the J. for Joel. His wife is given as Lucy Ann Mayberry or Mabery, & also as Lucretia Ann Mabry. Although these are undocumented assignments, the full Family story below lends some credence to them. The [1790] for VA contains both a Mabery family & a John Welbourn; the former in Pittsylvania Co & John in Powhaten Co. Heads of Families-Virginia, 1783. Image 106, Ancestry.com on-line database.

the FamilyTree claim of the Families' origin.

Owing principally to the comparatively late birth dates for this Family, the female contingent seems reasonably well established.

FORMAL GENEALOGY[2]

Generation 1

1. John Welborn[1], b <1765 d 183x m Lucy Ann maiden name presumably Mayberry or Mabery.[3]

Children of John[1] & Lucy Ann

+	2	i	Henry	b 1793
+	3	ii.	Marbury	b 1796
+	4	iii.	Abel Randel	b 1798
+	5	iv.	John	b 1806

---

[2] In this Formal Genealogy the Generations are calculated from the earliest progenitor, in keeping with suggested practice. The above Generation assignments are in keeping with Table One, Chapter One.

[3]   U. S. Census Wilkes Co NC

1810 John Wellborn household. Roll 43, p870, line 5.
1820 John Wellborn household. Roll 83, p515, line 18. Age class <1776.
1830 John Willbern household. Roll 125, p381, line 16. Age class 60-70, wife same. Near Abel R. & Henry.
1840 Lucy Wellborn household. Roll 373, p74, 4th from bottom. Age class 60-70. Widow, alone.
1870 Mary Wilborn household. Roll 1165, p356B, family 45 (blank on Schedule). This census presents some problems. With Mary are a Sarah 35 & another Mary 55, all bNC. These are identified below in Generation 2.

6   v.   *Mary*   *b 1806.*[4]

Generation 2

2.   Henry² (John¹), b 1793 in VA d ?186x   m Nancy
Redding b 1807 in 1821. Henry was a War of 1812 veteran: census
[1830, 1840, & 1860] all in Wilkes Co.[5]

Children of Henry² & Nancy

+	7.	i.	Henry	b 1829
+	8.	ii.	James R.	b 1834
+	9.	iii.	Thomas	b 1838

3.   Marbury² (John¹)   b 1796   d 1878   m2 Elizabeth
Green in 1815; Nancy Pritchett in 1862.

---

[4]   Parse [1810 1820] is a perfect fit for the sons; the daughter
b 1794-1804 is here assigned to Mary. Her only record is the [1870]
Wilkes, as head of household. U. S. census Wilkes Co NC, Mary
Wilborn household, Roll 1165, p356B, family 45 (blank entry on
Schedule). With her was Sarah daughter of Abel R & an unplaced Mary
age 55.

[5]   War of 1812, Service record, 7th Reg't, (Pearson's) North
Carolina Militia. M602, Roll box 227. Fide Ancestry.com on-line
database.
Marriage- Nancy Redding July 1821, bond Wm Redding.
FHL000546418/image 00324.
U. S. Census Wilkes Co NC
1830 Henry Wellburn household. Roll 125, p381, line 19. Age class 30-
40. Brother Abel R. nearby.
1840 Henry Wellborn household. Roll 373, p72, line 20. Age class 40-
50, Abel line 4.
1860 Henry Welborn household. Roll 918, p 23, family 323. Henry b
1793 VA, Nancy b NC 1807. Three sons, Henry b1819, James b1834,
Thomas b1838.
Parsing these three census accounts for all the sons, but the two
daughters remain unknown.

As Mabury Welborn he was a War of 1812 veteran serving as a youngster as a fifer, Pearsons 7th Reg't & later in Capt. Jas Martin's Co NC Militia. Records are [1820, thru 1860]: he left a Will in 1878 with his wife Nancy & all the children below as heirs.[6]

---

[6]   1812 Nancy applied for pension, no date given. Image of application on Ancestry.com on-line database: original numbers; Sur. Orig. 9193; Sur. Ctf. 15753; Wid. Orig. 23427; Wid. Ctf. 238868. The record as a fifer is from The War of 1812 Service Records, M602, roll box 226. Ancestry.com on-line database.
Marriage to Elizabeth Green, 29 Dec 1815. Bond by James Mabery ! North Carolina Marriage Bonds, 1741-1868, bond #000168003, record 02 264, printed version Wilkes County Marriage Bonds, p264, Ancestry.com on-line database. His second, & late, m to Nancy Pritchett in March of 1862: facsimile North Carolina Marriage Records, 1741-2011 from NC Register of Deeds, Record Group 48, NCDAH . Ancestry.com on-line database.
Will- Maberry Welborn /s/ 9/1876; probate 3/1878. Abstract from Book 6, folio 150 in Turner, Grace & Miles S. Philbeck, comps, Wilkes County North Carolina Will Abstracts, 1777-1910. By authors, Wilson Co., NC, 1988, #759.

U. S. Census Wilkes Co NC
1820 Mabery Willborn household. Roll 83, p529, line 1.
1830 Mayberry Wellborn household. Roll 125, p399, line 14
1840 Mabery Wellborn household. Roll 373, p27, line 18. This image 4, is not indexed by Ancestry.com.
1850 Mabery Willborn household. Roll 649, p265A, family 217. Age 54 bVA; Lucy 52 b Wilkes, Elizabeth 31 b Halifax. Adjacent families: John 22, & Allen 26. James M. appears in the Will but there are no records to be found.
1860 Mabery Wellborn household. Roll 918, p24, family 331. Age 64, no wife; Adlesy 25, presumably a relation– a daughter?
1870 Maberry Wilborne household. Roll 1165, p365B, family 165. Age 74, Nancy 50 & McWilliam 14.

Children of Marbury[2] & Elizabeth[7]

+	10.	i.	James M.	b 1816
+	11.	ii.	Allen Green	b 1822
+	12.	iii.	John O.	b 1827/8
	13.	iv.	Lucy Norman	b 1820
	14.	v.	Susannah Ashley	b 1825
	15.	vi.	Mary M. Penix	b 1829

4.   Abel Randel [2] **(John[1])**   b 1798/99 d 1855   m Patsey (Martha) Redden (Redding?) b1807 in 1824.
Occasionally went as Randel, e g his marriage to Patsey. Census: [1830,1840,1850]: he left a Will in 1855.[8]

---

[7] 1860 Yadkin Co NC, E. C. Norman household. Roll 919, p362, family 749. E. C. 40NC, Lucinda 40NC. The marriage record of Lewcinda (sic) to Early J. Norman in Jan of1855, Wilkes Co. Ancestry.com on-line database; original in North Carolina Marriage Indexes, NCSA. She elected to be known as Lucinda.
1860 Yadkin Co NC, Howell B. Ashley household. roll 919, p 334, family 327. H. B. 37NC, Susannah 35NC.
1870 Yadkin Co NC, William Penix household. roll 1592, p236A, family 79. Wm 48NC, Malisa 41NC. She apparently went by her middle name.

[8]   U.S. census Wilkes Co NC
1830 Abel R Willbern household.   Roll 125, p381, line14. Age class 30-40. Family group of father John & Henry.
1840 Abel R Wellborn household. Roll 373, p 72, lines 4 & 20. Near Henry & John.
1850 Randel Welborn household. Roll 649, p266A, family 228. b 12/1798 in VA, Martha b 1807 in Wilkes Co. Issue, Sarah 18, Martha 14, & John12. Son Joel is family 230.
1860 Martha Welborn household. Roll 918, p77(154), family 1101. Age 52; Sarah 28, John 20.
Will- June 1855, Book 5, folio 116. Turner, Grace & Miles S. Philbeck, comps, Wilkes County North Carolina Will Abstracts, 1777-1910. By authors, Wilson Co., NC, 1988, #754. Devisees Martha,

Children of Abel R². & Patsey

+	16.	i.	Joel A.	b 1827
	17.	ii.	Sarah L.	b 1832
	18.	iii.	Martha.	b 1836
+	19.	iv.	John M.	b 1838

Sarah & Martha are not in the Will.

5. **John² (John¹)** b 1806 d >188zz60 m Martha ?
All census [1840 thru 1880] In 1873, John age 66, submitted a claim before the Southern Claims Commission. He was accompanied by his brother Mabery & nephew Thos V. This sequence, on fold3, should be read by any surviving Family members as a long letter by John is included. This Family contained ten children, the most of any of Family G, & the parsing is complete for [1850 & 1860]. One female b 1830-1835 [1840] cannot be accounted for. Martha's maiden name is unknown.[9]

---

sons John M., Joel A. (Decd).

[9] U. S. Census Wilkes Co NC
1840 John Wellborn household. Roll 373, p74(28), 6th from bottom. Age class 30-40. Near Lucy Wellborn 60-70, his mother; 4th from bottom.
1850 John Willborn household. Roll 649, p278B, family 408. Listed are Lee D. 19, Mary 12, Lucinda 9, Mary Pearson 7; Willborns Abel 10, Francis 7, Malinda 6, Nancy 5, Henry 4, Sarah 2, John 1. A number of Pearson families are neighbors.
1860 John Welborn household. Roll 918, p77, family 1090. Listed Martha 47, Mary 22, Abel R. 21, Mary L. 20, Lucinda 19, Malinda 17, Nancy 15, Henry 18, Sarah L. 11, John 10.
1870 John Wilborn household. roll 1165, p357, family 50. John 63, Martha 58; John 20, Nancy 22, & Sarah 21.
1880 John Welborn household. Roll 987, p1830, family 184. Nancy E. 35, John 20 & daughter-in-law Mary A. & grandchildren.
fold3.com: Before the Commissioners of Claims. image 562530 et seq.

Children of John[2] & Martha

+	20.	i.	Lee D.	b 1831.
+	21.	ii.	Abel R.	b 1839
	22.	iii.	Mary	b 1838/1840
	23.	iv.	Lucinda	b 1841
	24.	v.	Francis	b 1843
	25.	vi.	Malinda	b 1844
	26.	vii.	Nancy	b 1845/1848
+	27.	viii.	Henry	b 1846
	28.	ix.	Sarah	b 1848/9
+	29.	x.	John	b 1849/50

Generation 3

7.   Henry M. [3] (Henry[2] , John[1]) b 1829 m Martha Jane Hampton 9/1866 in Wilkes Co d >1880. Census   with father & brothers in [1860], with Family [1880]. [10]

8.   James R.[3] (Henry[2], John[1]) b 1834 census [1870 1880] James Randel m Rebecca Felts 3/1865 Wilkes 03 057. issue 2 sons, 3daus.[11]

---

[10]   NC m records 03 057. NCDAH
U. S. Census Wilkes Co NC
1860 footnote 220
1880 Henry M Welborn household. Roll 987, p182A, family 155. Age 50, wife Martha J 31NC, three sons, one daughter.
Martha Jane Hampton Welborn b Feb 1829 d Dec 1926. Findagrave 78804382.

[11]   U. S. Census Wilkes Co NC
1870 James Willborn household. Roll 1165, p359A, family 83.
Rebecca 28.
1880 James R Wilborn household. Roll 987, p193A, family 153. A widower w/ two sons, three daughters.
James Randel m Rebecca Felts March 1865. NCDAH Marriage Files, Wilkes 03 057.

9.   Thomas V.[3] (Henry[2], John[1])   b 1838. m Fannie ?
Census [1880] with a Findagrave only. [12]

10.   James M. [3] (Marbury[2], John[1])   b 1816   d ?
James appears in his father's Will. There are seven pages of service
record in the NC 5th Senior Reserves, CSA available. He enrolled in
Yadkin Co in June of 1864 at age 48, and spent time in a hospital.[13]

11.   Allen Green[3] (Marbury[2], John[1])   b 1822   m
Martha ? d >1900.
Census [1850, 60, 80 ,1900]   No marriage record found.[14]

12.   John[3] (Marbury[2], John[1])   b 1827/8 m2
Adeliza ? b1830 Wilkes, Mary ? b1837   d 186x
In his farther's Will as John O. decd by 1876. Census [1850 1860]
only. [15]

---

[12]   U. S. Census Wilkes Co NC
1880 Thomas V Wilborn household. Roll 987, p184A, family 191. Age
42NC, Fannie V 37NC. Large family six sons, two daughters. Parents
all bNC. Next to cousin Allen G.
Findagrave #17014000.

[13]   Will, footnote 6.
fold3 images 31448068 et seq.

[14]   U. S. Census Wilkes Co NC
1850 Allen Wellborn household. Roll 649, p265B, family 219. Age 26
bWilkes; Martha 22 bWilkes. Family 219 is his brother John below.
1860 Allen Welborn household. Roll 918, p77, family 1094.
1880 Allen G. Welborn household. Roll 987, p184A, family 192.
Martha 53 bNC, Thomas M. 18 & nephew James F. 20. Also1900.

[15]   U. S. census Wilkes Co NC
1850 John Wellborn household. Roll 649, p265B, family 218. Age 22;
wife Adeliza age 20 b Wilkes.
1860 John Jr Wellborn household. Roll 918, p76 (153), family 1093.

16.   Joel A.[3] **(Abel R.**[2]**, John**[1]**)**   b 1827   m Nancy Hampton 1849 d between 1850 & 1855, the latter the date of his father's Will. footnote 8.   [1850] only.[16]

19.   John M.[3] **(Abel R.**[2]**, John**[1]**)**   b 1838 m?   d ? The only record so far is in father's [1850] age 12; footnote 8.

20.   Lee D.[3] **(John**[2]**, John**[1]**)**   b 1831   m Almedy (sic) ?   d 1918.
Census [1860, 1870, 1880]. His middle name is given as Davis in a Findagrave record. The [1860] is not in Ancestry.com's index. He was unmarried & living with a Dabney Parks: m later to Almeda ? & had issue. There are a number of frames for L. D. & Lee Davis in the military records of fold3. They establish residence in Iredell Co & indicate service in the CSA.[17]

21.   Abel R.[3] **(John**[2]**, John**[1]**)**   b 1839 d ?

Second wife Mary 23 bNC; next to brother Allen family 1094.
Will footnote 220.

[16] U. S. Census Wilkes Co NC
1850 Joel Wellborn household. Roll 649, p266, family 230. Age 23, Nancy 23 both b Wilkes.
M record image of bond April 1849 #6189, Ancestry.com on-line database.

[17]   U. S. census
1860 Wilkes Co NC, Dabney W. Parks household. roll 918 p 93 family 1812. Lee D. 27.
1870 Iredell Co NC, Davis Wilborn household. Roll 144, p141B.
1880 Iredell Co NC, Lee Welborn household. roll 968, p229C, ED 153.
Lee 48, Almedy (sic) 39, four sons, three daughters, the oldest 17.
Findagrave #73329237. Lee Davis Welborn, b 7/1831 d 6/1918.
Modern stone, New Hope Cemetery, Iredell Co NC.
fold3: L.D. Welborn, Iredell Co, petition for pardon. Image 24086610 et seq.

A letter to The Chairman, Oklahoma Board of Pension Commissioners, Oklahoma City, dated July 30, 1915 stipulates that Abel R. or A. R. Welborn was a sergeant in Company E, 54th NC Infantry. He enlisted in March of 1862 in Wilkes Co. Also a prisoner of War, paroled in March of 1864, but with no subsequent record.[18]

27.   Henry[3] (John[2], John[1])   b 1846   m?   d>1860
In [1860] he was still in his father's household. footnote 9 . No other information: a fold3 search turns up a Henry, but the information is not sufficient to specify this Henry.

29.   John3 (John[2], John[1])   b 1849/50   ? m Mary Byrd   d c1893.
This son, in some records as John Wesley, spent what must have been his entire life in his father's household. His last census [1880]. See   footnote 9   for all his census. His presumed marriage to Mary Byrd raises some issues: no marriage record can be found, albeit her death certificate claims John Wesley Welborn as spouse. In [1880] as Mary A. age 31 she is next to John in John Sr's household. But in [1900], as Mary A., she gives her d o b as February of 1852 & (most important) the number of years of marriage is left blank– with eight issue (of the marriage?). In [1910] her d o b is 1848, the years of m still blank & her issue still eight. A Findagrave record, #73917044, gives his vital data & Mary as wife, without a photo of a stone or other information. [19]

---

[18]   fold3 image #52459849. No Oklahoma records found.

[19]   U. S. census Wilkes Co NC
1900 Mary A. Welborn household. Roll 1224, p9B, family 172.
1910 Adna M Wilborn household. Roll 1135, p13B, family 237.

CHAPTER FOUR
Future Research– Unplaced or Unknown

Future Research– Unplaced or Unknown

There are four parts to this Chapter:
One– the existence of a 'Generation 0' individual: one that left sufficient records to establish his existence in The Old Granville District and to establish his relationship, if any, to The Families. (See Table One, p 2.)

Two– the possible existence of a family, with records that exist but do not fit any of the seven Families.

Three– records of individuals that cannot be subsumed in either of the above.

Four– miscellaneous notes.

PART ONE

There are a number of Rowan County records for a William, from 1758 to [1790], that must be accommodated. Perhaps the most important are that of a Regulator c1761. In 1762 there are two records: a road construction assignment & the acquisition of 700A of land, both in Abbotts Creek.[1] These records, most importantly, predate William B2 (b1761) as an adult.

There are three Rowan Co [1790]– for two Williams & a James, discussed in Chapter Three pps 69 & 84. These are part of a Family B group– all are b<1775– including Progenitor James & his sons Isaac, Gideon, & William. Generation 3 is represented by

---

[1]   Wheeler, John, H., Historical Sketches of North Carolina, 1584-1851. GPC (Clearfield) 1993 (1825).
MARS ids 12.13.120.25 & 12.12.76.34.

Isaac Jr & William Jr.[2]

A genealogist for Family B maintains the early William was father to James B1.[3] Records, moreover, give credence to this assertion: William b c1708 & Thomas b c1701 were sons of Edward Wilbourn of MD.[4] James B1's first NC record was 1752 in Anson Co and/or 1759 in Rowan & the [1790]. Accounting for the three Generations in the [1790] & the fact that in James' household, two males b<1775 were listed suggests that William 'B0', (b1708) & son of Edward, was residing with his son. Although there is no direct evidence, the simultaneous presence of both in Rowan Co with the age difference provides the basis for assigning William 'B0' as the father of Progenitor James.

Although not within the scope of the present Book, another very possible ' Generation 0 ' was a John Wellburn who served as a private in The Continental Line, & whose heirs (unspecified) were rewarded land in TN (then as part of NC) in 1791. He was recorded then as deceased. [5]

PART TWO

John Wilkes (one of a number of Family members with the middle name of Wilkes) might well belong to an eighth Family in the Old Granville District. He can provisionally be assigned the son of

---

[2]   U. S. census
1790 Rowan/Salisbury, James Wilborn household. Roll 7, p322, age distribution 2/3/4. The Family entries are amongst the bottom 14 lines.

[3]   Welborn, Gene, Welborns and related families with roots in North and South Carolina. By author, Greenwood SC,1994. The author provides no documentation for this link.

[4]   Barnes , Robert W., Baltimore County Families 1659-1759. GPC 1989, pps 690,702

[5]   MARS Id 12.14.2.1716, S.108.358.

a William Welborn of Orange County– a William not included in those treated in Chapter Two. The assignment is the result of a parse of an [1820] Orange Co, but with other & conflicting evidence.

John Wilkes Wilburn b 2/1809 in Orange Co NC, d 3/1878 in Cooke Co TX. A Findagrave for him has a brief biography including vital, marriage & issue– information that is corroborated by census & marriage record. Census [1830] Marion Co IL has a John & Peter W. Wilborn in adjacent households, both 20-30, strongly suggesting the two are brothers. Peter W. has his own Findagrave, providing additional information.[6]

Parsing the William of Orange County would assign John W. to the 10-15 year old, & Peter W. to the 16-18 one.
John W. m 1831 Martha Susan Deadmond in Marion IL: Susan indicated as his wife in all census, b VA in 1813. (Peter m a sister, Jerusha Deadmond.)

----

[6]   findagrave #11358209. Original stone. Added material says he was a Doctor as do later census. b Feb 11, 1809 of William Wilbourn & Mary "Molly" Wilkes of Orange Co. NC; d March 12, 1878 in Cooke Co TX. Burial Marysville Cemetery, Cooke Co TX. findagrave #11351697 Peter W. Wilbourn b Feb 15, 1803 in Lynchburg City VA; d Nov 12, 1857 in Marion Co IL. spouses Jerusha Deadmond & Cynthia Scott. Both of the Findagraves are contributed by the same individual-- the two fit together & are consistent with the census. In William's 1820 census, both Peter & John parse (underlined in footnote. The Lynchburg VA connection needs support, however. see the census exploration for William.
    U. S. census
1820 Orange Co NC, Wm Wilborn household. Roll 82, p402, line 11. males <10, 10-15, (16-18), 16-25; 5f, wife.
1830 Marion Co IL, John Wilborn household. Roll 22, p194, line 5. Age class 20-30. Next line is Peter W. Wilborn, same age class.
1850 Grayson Co TX, Jno Wilburn household. Roll 910, p341A, family 50. Age 41 bNC, Susan 37VA. Occupation Physician.
1860 Grayson Co TX, J. W. Wilbourn household. Roll 1295, p171, family 497. Age 57, occupation Physician. Susan 47VA.
1870 Cook Co TX, John W. Wilburn household. Roll 1580, p233B, family 9. Age 61 bNC, Susan 57 bVA.

While in IL John W. purchased 40A Feb 14, 1839, selling it a year later before moving to TX. [7]
Although the information on John W. & Peter W. Wilbourn seems complete enough, the assignment of William of Orange Co as their father depends upon a parse & information in the Findagraves.
Records of William in Orange Co are problematic. From 1761 & 1764 land records for a William W- are clear enough, but the next record found is in 1811, a gap of some 50 years too long to afford convincing evidence that the same William was involved.[8] The next record, chronologically, is the [1820], footnote above.

There is an Orange Co Estate file for William Wilbourn dated 1822. In that File is a facsimile copy of a petition, translated here:
Orange Co. Image 11
> To the Worshipful the Justice of the Court of Pleas & Quarter Sessions for Orange County - The petition of Nancy Wellborn. Exporte
> Humby herewith unto your Worship, your petitioner

---

[7]   John Wilbourn - Susan Deadmond, m Oct 6, 1831, Marion IL. FHL mfilm 1010815. John Wilbourn, 40A, County not explicit, ID #205723; IL Public Land Purchase Records, 1813-1909. Ancestry.com On-line database. Sale of this land in Sept of 1840 land, Marion Co IL, was to Isaac Andrick, fide Deadmond   family bible, rootsweb.ancestry.com/~okgs/deadmond_wilbourne_records.htm.]

[8]   Land records MARS 12.12.68.3, Warrant April 3, 1761 700A on McEntire Creek, Deep River, Orange Co. This drainage is located today in Randolph Co, DeLorme Atlas p 37, panel C1.
MARS 12.14.95.267, 270A patent & 375 A, 1761. It is not clear that these apply to the same land.
1764 Court filing of deed transfer of Thomas to Wm Wilburn, Weeks, Eve B., trans, Register of Orange County, North Carolina Deeds- 1752-1768 & 1793. Heritage Papers, Danielsville GA, 1984 , p30.]

Nancy Wellburn of Orange County that William Willburn late of said County departed this life on the 8th Day of October in the present year, Intestate, and he left your petitioner, his widow surviving him, with a Family of seven children. Your petitioner shews (?) that her late said husband was possessed at the time of his death of [?] personal Estate, whence of Letters of Administration have been by your Worship at this present term granted Joseph Wood who hath undertaken the Burdens of the [?] : Your petitioner further shows that she is entitled to a adequate provision for the support of herself and said family for one year to be [?] alloted [?] out of the Crop?, [?] & provisions left on hand by her husband: and to the end that such allotment be made & that she be let in the enjoyment thereof. She humbly prays your Worship & appointed one Justice of the Peace thru [?] qualified according to law, who shall view the said Estate & make the said allotment on Oath & return the same under this hand & seal with this Court at the next term thereof, pursueing in all in [?] the directions contained in the Acts of the General Assembly in such case made & provided: and your petitioner with ever prayers. /s/ Nancy Wilburn. [9]

The problem of assigning this petition to the aforesaid William of Orange Co is that the William's wife was apparently not Nancy, but Mary "Molly" – at least according to the Findagrave information. In addition, she claims seven children: the [1820] for William indicates a total of nine; four males & five females.

We are thus left with a total of contradictory information. While the evidence for John Wilkes & Peter Wilkes Wilbourn is convincing, assigning them to the William of Orange County NC will

---

[9]   North Carolina Estate Files, 1663-1979, Orange County, North Carolina, 1822., index & images, FamilySearch, FHL mfilm 002069373. The petition is image 11.

require further investigation.

PART THREE

Individuals w/o any assignment or conclusions.

Acquila Welborn. There are three records, before 1776, that may pertain to the same individual although they are in three different locations. They are not that far apart, but some follow-up work must be done to determine if a single Acquila is involved. (Acquila B3, son of Gideon was b1794.) [10]

Rebecka Wellborn   m William Morgan, Wilkes Co in July of 1814. Her age probably places her in Generation 3. A William B. Morgan is found in Carter Co TN, with a wife Rebecca. However, she gives her age as 44 ! [11] Age 54 would be commensurate with her m record. If the same woman, which seems likely, she may have been the daughter of Gideon (of Wilkes Co)

Gideon Wilborn b c1765   d ?

There are three land and a single census for this Gideon in Wilkes, to become Ashe Co. Gideon B2's records were in Rowan Co & Barren Co KY. [12]

---

[10]   Acquila Welborn is listed amongst the debtors of Col McGee's Ordinary, 1773. NCGJ v1, #1 p38ff.

The same year, in Guilford Co, Acquila Welborn /s/ a petition for the Courthouse location. RCGJ x, pps 33-37.

Surry-Wilkes taxables list included a Aquller (sic) Wilborn, one white poll, 1775, Benj Cleavelands regt. Johnson, William Perry, Surry-Wilkes Counties Taxables, 1771-1800. by author, Raleigh 1974, p32.

[11]   U S census

1850 Carter Co TN, William B. Morgan household. Roll 873, p 164A family 4. Age 55 bNC, Rebecca 44NC; oldest son age25 bNC.

M record- Ancestry.com on-line database. Original NCDAH record group 048.

[12]   The earliest record is in 1787 whence Joseph Crouch enters 200A on the VA line including some of the waters of Little

Harrison C. A. Welborn b 1818NC m Millie Harris in 1850, Dobson NC. Resided Surry Co & later moved to IA – he does not fit any parse in Family F. The clear relationship to the Naylor family needs clarification: it is quite possible he was illegitimate.[13]

John Wilbourn of Orange Co NC; b<1756 m? d 1819. This John left only three records, had no issue & died in debt. He must have been one of the earliest W-s in The District, so he may have been related to one the Family Progenitors. [14]

Hinton Creek. This property is recorded on MARSid 12.14.124.1168 & 1162. On Grassy Creek, New River he acquired more land 1791- MARSid 12.14.14.1667 & in 1799 when Ashe Co was formed, 94A more, Grassy Creek; MARSid 12.14.28.177.
    U. S. census
1800 Ashe Co NC, Gideon Wilborn household. Roll 29, p91, line6. Age class 1755- 1774.

[13]   U. S. census
1850 Surry Co NC, Naylor family household. Roll 646, p183A, family 329. Harrison age 26.
1860 Yadkin Co NC, Harrison C. A. household. Roll 919, p355, family 650. Age 35, Mildred 45, both bNC.
1870 Poweshiek IA, Harrison ? household. Roll 417, p433A, family 93. Age 50. Next to Naylors.
M 1850 Harrison C.A. to Milly Harris. Dobson County Court Records, FHL 0546467-74.
1879, Findagrave #7669848. Poweshiek IA. Vital b 4/1818 d 7/1879. Good readable stone, inscription 'age 61y, 8m, 14d'.

[14]   U. S. census
1790 Orange Co NC, John Wilbern. This record is not from the regular [1790], but presumably from a tax list. The Federal Schedule for Orange Co was either not taken or lost. Ancestry.com presents an Index Only listing w/Roll 7 & p96 that cannot be found or searched. Anc. refers to FHL mfilm #0568147. The Heads of Families Booklet for the First U.S. census (GPC 1973) does list John on p96– there is no age distribution.

Jesse Welborn   b c1800   d ?

There are in the DataBase nine records of this Jesse, all in Randolph Co & all court records. Nearly all are for presentments or complaints. (Two were in Criminal Court). Clearly Jesse was in trouble with the Law from 1818 (the first) thru 1840. The problem is to determine to which Family he belongs. There are no census– & no records in Ancestry.com on-line database. All records appear in The RCGJ in various years. Perhaps a clue is that in the 1840 Criminal Court proceedings, on a charge of assault, Joseph Welborn appears as guardian– almost certainly Joseph A3.[15]

PART FOUR

NOTES - refer to p75, footnote 18.

The [1820] for Guilford Co has no W-s. In [1830] Guilford, however, there are two W- entries that require some scrutiny:

1800 Orange Co NC, John Wilbourn household. Roll 34, p605, line 4. A couple b<1756 w/ no family.

North Carolina Estate Files, 1663-1979. John Wilbourn, 1819 Orange Co. There are 28 images available, all having to do with sales to pay off his debts: no Welbourn names were recorded. Available FamilySearch.

[15]   Selected:

1818 Jesse Welborn, presentment for committing an affray. RCGJ XXVII(4), (2003), p22.

1823 Jesse Willborn, presentment. RCGJ XXIX(1), (2005).

1832 Jesse Wellborn (inter alia) Presentment on a charge of stealing. RCGJ XXX(3), (2006), p17.

1833 Jesse Welborn, Bill of Complaint by Howgill Julian, ibid, p19.

1836 Jesse Welborn, charge of assault on G. Cousins. RGCGJ XXXII(1), p6. (2008)

1840 Jesse Welborn, Criminal Court on a charge of assault. Joseph Welborn guardian. RGGJ XXXIII (2009), p44. (The same appeared earlier in vol II (1978)).

1840 Jesse Welborn & Jesse Watkins on a charge of fighting. ibid.

Ancestry.com, presumably based upon some name index, gives one as Moses & the other as Mons translated as Moris. Examination of the magnified pages strongly indicates that the enroller intended the names to be identical. Neither of the entries looks to the eye as 'Moses', but placed side-by-side they are identical (& on different pages). Perusal of the Schedule's pages reveals other entries of orthography identical to the two Welbourns. When the [1820] is searched one such entry, for a Mendenhall, proves to be a clearly-written Moses. All this indicates that the [1830] enroller, in spite of a curious 'hand', intended the two W-s to be Moseses.

In addition, the age distribution of the males in the two families is quite different– although the female contingent is the same. A look at the Family parsing mentioned in Chapter Three suggests only two possibilities for the four Welborns above. One of these is Isaac B2 who died intestate in MO about 1824. A difficulty here is that the crucial [1820] for him is missing. The other is the Moses with the [1830] age distribution of sons that can accommodate four in the necessary range 1815-1820. A tentative, but persuasive, conclusion is that the four Lafayette W-s were of a Moses– for whom we have no other information but the [1830] in Guilford Co NC.

NOTES- refer to p88 for Samuel B2.
The text reads that census indicates he had a 2nd wife. The material here suggests that she was a Lydia, maiden name unknown.
In [1840 & 1850] a Lydia W- was enrolled in IN. In the latter, the household consisted of Lydia Welburn, age 74 bNC; William 50 bNC; and Sarah 40 bKY. (The [1840] for Liddy Wilbern listed a single male 30-40, & females 5-10, 10-15, & 60-70.) These lead to a check of [1810] in KY & presumably also in [1820 & 1830].
A parsing of all KY W-s in those latter two census point to Samuel B2 as the **only** KY W- that fulfills the requirements of a male (William) b1800 & a female (Sarah) b 1810. Thus we conclude that Samuel m again, a Lydia ? sometime before 1820, & that she

undoubtedly brought children to the Family.[16]

Notes- refer to Chapter One, p2.
Occasional FamilyTree contributors have maintained that some of the seven Progenitors were brothers, although no hard evidence was provided. Such seems circumstantial as the congregation of the W-s in The Old Granville District when the lands opened up in the mid-eighteenth Century was, perhaps, remarkable. And, for example, three land acquisition records from 1761 & 1762 involve three of the Progenitor's names in common. Where they related or simply neighbors? Research in VA & MD will need to be done to establish the answer. [17]

---

[16]   U. S. census
1810 Barren Co KY, Samuel Wilbourn household. Roll 5, p46, line 16. Family distribution includes males 26-44, **<10** & 10-15, females 26-44, 3<10, 10-15.
1820 Cumberland Co KY, Samuel Wilbourn household. Roll 19, p159, line 4 bottom page. Family consists of eight males ranging from <10 to (two) b<1776, (including one b **1794-1804**); & five females, **3<10.** Such suggests a merging of two families.
1830 Russell Co KY, Samuel Wilbourn household. Roll 41, p122, line 5th from bottom. The age distribution accommodates a male age 20 & a female age 20.
1840 Owen Co IN, Liddy Wilbern household. Roll 89, p84, line 4. Males 30-40 (William) & females 5-10, 10-15, 60-70.
1850 Greene Co IN, Lydia Wilburn household. Roll 148, p352A, family 1025. Son William b1800NC & daughter Sarah b 1810KY.

[17]   From vol 3 of Hofmann, Margaret M., The Granville District of North Carolina 1748-1763. Version pub 1989 by author, Ahoskia NC.
#2273, p57. Thomas Welborne, 225A Orange Co Sandy Run, Oct 2nd 1761. Witness Wiliam Welborn.
#2259, p55. Edward Wellborn, 425A Orange Co Sandy Run, Jun 30th 1762. Chain carriers William & Thomas Welborn.
#2275, p57. Thomas Welborne, 225A Orange Co Sandy Run, Oct 2nd 1761. Witness William Welborn.

A start would be in two sources; Robert Barnes, Baltimore County Families 1659-1759, GPC 1989 & Jane Baldwin, Maryland Calendar of Wills, Family Line 1988. These two, e g, have William Wilbourn (B0 above), b c1708, m Ann Crabtree in 1731 the parents of William (C1) b 1734 & James (C1) b 1736. See also p67.

INDEX & APPENDICES

INDEX Welborn males

	Family	Parent	Pages		
Aaron	B2	James	81		
Aaron	B3	Aaron	84	91	
Aaron	B3	James jr	83	86	97
Abel R	G4	John	176	179	
Abel R(andel)	G3	John J.	174		
Abner	C2	William	107	113	
Abner	C3	Elias	110	118	
Acquila	B3	Gideon	88	99	
Allen G.	G4	Maberry		174	177
Barnabas	B3	William	85	96	
Carter T.	B3	James jr	86	98	
Cary	B3	William	85	94	
Caleph	A2	Thomas	57		
Chapley	B3	James jr	86	98	
Chapley R	C2	William	107	114	
Cyrus	A4	Wm3	64		
Daniel	F2	Isaac	161	164	
Daniel Jr	F3	James	166		
Daniel	E3	Lewis	147		
Daniel H	F3	Daniel	165	167	
David	D4	Elias	128	134	
David L	A4	Jos3	65		
David M	F3	Samuel	165		
Davis	B3	William	85	94	
Edward	E1		4	137	143
Edward	E2	Edward	144	148	
Edward	E3	Thomas	146	150	
Elias	C2	William	106	109	
Elias	C3	Isaac	108	115	
Elias	D3	John	126	127	
Elias jr	D4	Elias	128	129	
Elijah	A2	Thomas	60		
Elisha	B3	Aaron	92		
Elisha	B3	Samuel not in Book			
Elisha (Elijah)	A4	Jos3	64		
Emsley	D4	Elias	128	129	
Enoch	D3	John	126	129	

194

Enoch E.	D4	Jesse Y	127	133	
Ephreim	A2	Thomas	60		
Evans	A4	John3	62		
Ezekiel	A2	Thomas	61		
F. Montgomery	F3	Daniel	165	16	
Frederick D	A4	Jos3	65		
George W.	D4	Elias	128	134	
George Y.	D4	JesseY	127	132	
Gideon jr	B3	Aaron	84	92	
Gideon	B2	James	81	86	
Gideon	U		187		
Harrison C.A.	U		186		
Henry	G3	John J.	172		
Henry	G4	John	176	179	
Henry H.	D4	Elias	128	134	
Henry M	G4	Henry	176		
Hugh M	C3	James	112	119	
Isaac Jr	B2	James	25	81	
Isaac	B3	Isaac2	25	82	90
Isaac	C2	William	25	106	107
Isaac	D3	John	25	126	129
Isaac	F1		4	153	160
Isaac	F2	Isaac	25	161	162
Isaac	F3	Samuel	25	165	
Isaac jr	C3	Isaac	25	108	115
Isaac P	B3	William	25	85	96
Jacob	B3	Joshua	89	101	
James	B1		4	67	79
James	B2	James	37	81	85
James	B3	Samuel	37	88	100
James	B3	Aaron	37	84	90
James	B3	James jr	37	86	
James	C2	William	37	106	
James	C3	Isaac	37	108	114
James	D3	John	37		
James	E3	Lewis	37	147	151
James	F2	Isaac	37	161	164
James	F3	James	37	166	
James H.	D4	John	129	135	
James J	C3	James	37	112	119
James M	B3	John	90	102	

James M.	G4	Maberry		175	177	
James Madison	C3	Elias	37	118		
James R.	G4	Henry	176			
James W(ood)	A4	John3	63			
James W.	F3	Daniel				
James W.	D4	JesseY				
Jesse	A3	Jhn2	58			
Jesse	A4	Wm3	6			
Jesse	B3	Samuel	88	100		
Jesse H. same	D4	Jesse Y	127	132		
Jesse M same	A4	John3				
Jesse Y	D3	John	126	127		
Jesse	U		187			
Joel A.	G4	Abel R	175	178		
John	A2	Thomas	14	58		
John	A3	John2	14	58	62	
John	A4	John3	62			
John	A4	Isaac3	62			
John	B2	James	14	81	89	
John	B3	John	14	90	102	
John W.	C3	Samuel	111	118		
John	D2		4	14	121	125
John	D3	John	14	126	128	
John	D4	Isaac	129	136		
John (M)	D4	Elias	128	134		
John C.	D4	Jesse Y	127	131		
John	E2	Edward	14	144	145	
John	F2	Isaac	14	161	162	
John J	G2		14	170	171	
John	G3	John J.	14	175		
John M.	G4	Abel R	175	178		
John O.	G4	Maberry		174	177	
John	G4	John	176	179		
John, Wilkes			183			
Johnson	C2	William	107	113		
Joseph	A3	Jhn2	58	64		
Joseph	D4	John	129	135		
Joseph O.P.	A4	Wm3	63			
Joshua	A2	Thomas	59			
Joshua jr	B3	Joshua	89	100		
Joshua	B2	James	81	89		

196

Joshua	D4	JesseY	127	131	
Lee D	G4	John	176	178	
Levi	D4	William	127	130	
Lewis	E2	Edward	144	145	147
Lewis J	F3	James	166		
Lewis Jr	E4	Lewis	150		
Linden McGee	A4	Jos3	65		
Logan	A4	John3	63		
Maberry	G3	John J.	172		
Marshall H	C3	Elias	109	117	
Moses	B2	James	72	81	82
Moses	B3	Moses	75	90	
Moses	B3	William	74	85	95
Moses	B3	James jr	76	86	96
Parsons	A4	John3	62		
Peter Wilkes			184		
Richard	E2	Edward	144	148	
Richard Jr	E3	Richard	148		
Richard	E3	Lewis	149	151	
Robert	E3	Richard	149		
Robert	E3	Thomas	146		
Robert Mc	A4	Jos3	65		
Samuel	F2	Isaac	48	161	163
Samuel	B3	William	48	85	93
Samuel Col	C2	William	48	106	110
Samuel	B2	James	48	81	88
Samuel Jr	B3	Samuel	48	88	99
Samuel C	C3	James	48	112	119
Samuel jr	C3	Samuel	48	110	118
Shelton	C3	Isaac	109	116	
Stearns	C3	Isaac	109	116	
Stephen	C3	Elias	109	118	
Terry Scott	A4	John3	62		
Thomas	A1		4	54	57
Thomas	A2	Thomas	43	60	
Thomas	B3	William	43	85	95
Thomas	B3	Aaron	43	84	91
Thomas	B3	James jr	43	86	97
Thomas	E2	Edward	43	144	145
Thomas S	F3	Daniel	43	165	168
Thomas V	G4	Henry	177		

Thompson	B3	Gideon	88	99	
Wiley K	A4	John3	63		
Wilkes	C2	William	107	114	
William	A2	Thomas	25	61	
William L.	A3	John2	25	58	63
William J	A4	John3	62		
William L	A4	Joseph3	64		
William	'B0'		182		
William	B2	James	25	81	84
William	B3	James jr	25	86	97
William F	B4	Isaac			
William	B3	Gideon	25	88	99
William	B3	Joshua	25	89	101
William	C1		4	103	106
William Jr	C2	William	25	107	112
William Wilkes	C3	James	25	112	119
William	C3	Isaac	25	109	115
William	D3	John	25	126	
William	D4	John	129	135	
William	D4	William Wm has Levi only			
William	D4	Isaac	129	136	
William W.	D4	JesseY	127	132	
William	E3	Edward	25	151	
William	F2	Isaac	25	160	161
William jr	F3	Samuel	25	165	
William	U		184		
Wisdom	B3	William	85	96	
Wm Ruffin	A4	Wm3	63		
Younger	B3	Aaron	84		
Zachariah	E2	Edward	144	146	

Duckworth	Anna	dB2	Aaron	84	90
Duckworth	Ruth	dB2	Aaron	84	91
Edwards	Lydia	dB3	John	90	
Edwards	Rebecca	dB3	John	90	
Elzey	Martha Elzey	wB3	Gideon	92	
Farlow	Martha Jane	dA3	Joseph	65	
Felts	Rebecca Felts	wG3	James R.	176	
Fentress	Mary Ann	dA3	Joseph	64	
Fleming	Mary	dC2	Elias	110	
Franklin	Rebecca M.	dC2	James	112	
Franklin	Ann P. Franklin	wC3	William Jr.	119	
Gallimore	Susannah	dA2	John	58	
Gardner	Nancy	dA3	Wiliam	64	
Gray	Martha (1st)	dA2	John	62	
Green	Elizabeth Green	wG2	Marbury (1st)	172	
Griggs	Francis Griggs	wB3	Jacob	101	
Halbert	Sarah Halbert	wB3	Moses	96	
Hampton	Mary Hampton	wE2	John	145	
Hampton	Mary J. Hampton	wG3	Henry M.	176	
Hampton	Nancy Hampton	wG3	Joel A.	178	
Hanner	Esther	dA3	J. Hanner	58	
Hanner	Martha M	dA3	William	64	
Harris	Milly Harris	wU	Harrison C.A.	186	
Hayworth	Hannah Haworth	wB3	Davis	94	
Hayworth	Isabel	dB3	John	90	
Healey	Phoebe Healey	wD4	Joshua	131	
Hinshaw	Eliz. Ellen	dA3	Joseph	65	
Hilton	Martha	dA3	John	62	
Hill	Selenia	dC2	Elias	110	
Hitchcock	Jemima Hitchcock	wB3	Barabas	96	
Horney	Sarah Horney	wB3	James M.	102	
Hudlow	Mary J. Hudlow	wD3	David	134	
Jones	Susannah	dE1	Edward	144	
Killon	Rebeckah	dF1	John J.	156	163
King	Nancy	dC2	Isaac	109	
Lacey	Martha Lacey	wA3	William	63	
Ledbetter	Betsy A	dC2	James	112	
Lewis	Lucy	dC2	Elias	109	
Loftis	Jane	dE1	Edward	144	
Marbury	Lucy A. Marbury	wG1	John J.	171	
Marshall	Temperance	dE1	Edward	144	

Marshall	Mary Marshall	wC2	Elias	109	
Martin	Nancy Martin	wC3	Hugh M.	119	
Martin	Mary (P) Martin	wB3	Thomas	91	
Matkin	Jemima Matkin	wB3	Isaac Jr.	90	
McGee	Jane McGee	wA2	John	54	
McNairy	Elizabeth Jane	dA3	James M.	63	
Meredith	Choicy	dB3	John	90	
Miller	Elizabeth	dD2	Elias	128	
Mills	Nancy Mills	wD3	Joseph	135	
Montgomery	Cristine M.	wF3	William	160	
Montgomery	Rebecca M.	wC2	James M.	105	111
Moore	Mary Moore	wD3	James H.	135	
Moore	Lucy H. Moore	wC2	William	112	118
Mullen	Martha (2nd)	dA2	John	62	
Nichols	Mary E. Nichols	wB3	Isaac P.	96	
Norman	Lucy	dG3	Marbury	174	
Norman	Lucinda	dG2	John	176	
Parks	Katherine S	dC2	James	112	
Parsons	Mary Parsons	wA3	John (1st)	62	
Parsons	Ruth	dB1	James	81	
Payne	Mary Eliza Payne	wB3	John (2nd)	102	
Payne	Rachel Payne	wB2	William (1st)	84	
Payne	Margaret	dB3	John	89	
Penix	Mary M.	dG2	Marbury	174	
Pritchett	Nancy	wG2	Marbury (2nd)	172	
Ramsour	Elizabeth	dA2	John	59	
Redding	Nancy Redding	wG2	Henry	172	
Redding	Patsey Redding	wG2	Abel R.	174	
Render	Martha Render	wC2	Abner	113	
Render	Sallie Render	wC2	Johnson	113	
Robbins	Jane	dA3	John	62	
Roberts	Susannah Roberts	wE3	Richard	148	
Roundtree	Mary Roundtree	wA2	Elijah	61	
Saxton	Parthena Saxton	wA3	Joseph	64	
Simmons	Edith Simmons	wA3	Jesse	65	
Skinner	Nancy	dD2	Elias	128	
Slaughter	Lydia=Lida	dE1	Edward	144	
Small	Eleanor	dD2	Elias	128	
Smith	Rachel Smith	wB2	Joshua	89	
Starnes	Mary Starnes	wC3	Samuel C. (1st)	119	
Stearnes	Nancy M	dC2	James	112	

Stearns	Hepzebah Stearns	wC1	William	103	106
Stevenson	Lucy Stevenson	wB3	Aaron	91	
Stovall	Tabitha Stovall	wB2	Gideon	86	
Swafford	Elenor Swafford	wD2	Elias	128	
Swafford	Margaret	dD2	Elias	128	
Swaim	Elizabeth	dF1	John	161	
Swaim	Sarah J	dA3	Joseph	65	
Swift	Elizabeth A.	dB1	James	81	
Talbert	Deress	dD2	Elias	128	
Teague	Martha Teague	wB2	Moses	82	
Teague	Lydia Teague	wB2	John W.	89	
Teague	Mary I. Teague	wB1	James	79	
Templeton	Mary A. T.	wF3	Thomas F.	168	
Tillman	Ann P. Tillman	wC3	Elias	115	
Tomlinson	Elvira Tomlinson	wF2	Isaac	162	
Wadell	Nancy Wadell	wB3	Wiliam	98	
Watson	Susan M. Watson	wF3	Lewis	166	
Welborn	Abagail	dB2	John	90	
Welborn	Amy	dA1	Thomas	57	
Welborn	Anna	dB1	James	81	
Welborn	Catherine	dF2	Daniel	165	
Welborn	Francis	dG2	John	176	
Welborn	Lucinda	dG2	John	176	
Welborn	Malinda	dG2	John	176	
Welborn	Martha	dG2	Abel R.	175	
Welborn	Martha E.	dF2	Daniel	165	
Welborn	Mary	dG2	John	176	
Welborn	Nancy	dG2	John	176	
Welborn	Polly	dC2?	??	117	
Wellborn	Polly	dC2	?	117	
Welborn	Rebecca	dF2	James	164	167
Welborn	Ruth	dA1	?	57	
Welborn	Sally Eliza	dA3	?	63	
Welborn	Sarah L.	dG2	Abel R.	175	
Welborn	Sarah York	dG2	John	176	
Welborn	Susan S.	dF2	?	165	
Welch	Elizabeth	dB2	William	85	
White	Jemima White	wE2	Zachariah	146	
White	Anne	dD2	John	126	
Wiley	Nancy	dC1	William 107	114	
Wilson	Elizabeth Wilson	wB3	Acquila	99	

Wood	Priscilla Wood	wA3	John (2nd)	62	
Wright	Martha	dD2	John	126	
York	Sarah York	wD2	John	121	125
Younger	Rebecca Younger	wB2	James Jr	85	
Younger	Elizabeth Younger	wB2	Aaron	83	

APPENDIX ONE

The Database

There are three main Spreadsheet folders that contain the material assembled over the years. Each is sorted in various ways– e g census appears as name; year; & State & County.

1- Federal & State census, both Population Schedule & Agriculture as appropriate, from [1790] thru [1880]. There are 698 entries– regardless of their occurrence in 2- & 3-.

2- A Master File that includes all information (land, petition, probate, court, &   ) by individual. Limited census is included for critical identification purposes. Currently this Spreadsheet contains 1702 entries of information.

3- A Roster File containing every individual appearing in The Book, with Family affiliation. There are 292, to date. Also included are individuals unplaced– Chapter Four.

APPENDIX TWO

References

General

North Carolina Department of Archives & History.
   Estate Records, Randolph Co. 081.508.
   Estate Records, Rowan/Davidson Cos. 085.508.144.

North Carolina Department of Archives & History.
   Marriage Files   Co Code   #

North Carolina Department of Archives & History.
   Estate Records, Randolph County 081.508.
   Estate Records, Rowan/Davidson Counties 085.508.144.

North Carolina, Estate Files, 1663-1979," index and images, FamilySearch (https://familysearch.org/pal:/MM9.1.1/QJ8L-11L7 : accessed 22 Sep 2014), FHL microfilm 002069373.

Saint Francois County, Missouri History and Biographies, pub by Mountain Press, Signal Mountain TN, 2006. p81. This reference is a copy of a work published in about 1889 (from the dates included in the text) that Mountain Press does not explicitly acknowledge– while providing information one wishes for better documentation.

Saint Francois County Records same Publisher & date.

Family bible
Genealogical data from bibles in the possession of the North Carolina Historical Commission. Transcribed by The North Carolina DAR. Family History Library Catalog. FHL US/CAN Film 18067, item 3.

Military
Muster Rolls of the Soldiers of the War of 1812: detached from The Militia of North Carolina, in 1812 and 1814. Pub. By the General Assembly January 21, 1851. Reprinted GPC 1980.

Census
 U.S. census, name of , place, pop sch, , roll ##, page ##, line #

Commercial
Ancestry.com; On-line database– searchable

Ancestry.com. Source. List of taxable property in Rowan County NC 1778. Indexed by Annie W. Burns.

Books & Periodicals
Absher, Mrs W. O., Wilkes County North Carolina Will Abstracts, 1781-1811. Southern Historical Press, Easley SC, 1989.

Absher, Mrs W.O., Surry County, North Carolina deed abstracts. Books D,E, & F, 1779-1797. Southern Historical Press, Easley SC, 1985.

Alexander, V., C.M. Elliott, & B. Willie, Pendleton District and Anderson Counties, South Carolina Wills, Estates, Inventories, Tax and Census records. Southern Historical Press, Easley, 1980. [Thomas W. Will p158. Wife mary, sons Wm Thos, Aaron, James. Exctrs James, Aaron, probate 28/8/1868.]

Austin, Jeanette H., Georgia Bible Records, GPC 1985.

Bailey, Pat Shaw, Land Grants Records of North Carolina, vol I Orange County 1752-1885. Pub. by author, Graham N.C., 1990.

Bennnett, William D. Ed., Orange County Records. Vols 1-14. My notes- By author Rocky Mount 1990.(LOC 1987 Raleigh) Or Guilford County Deed Book One. By author, Raleigh 1990.(LOC)

Blair, J. A., Reminiscences of Randolph County, North Carolina. By author, Asheboro 1890.

Blair, Ruth, Some Early Tax Digests of Georgia. GA Dept. Archives & History, 1926-reprint 1971.

Bockstruck, Lloyd deWitt, Revolutionary War Pensions. GPC, 2011.

Bowen, Eliza A., The Story of Wilkes County Georgia. Clearfield (GPC) reprint 1997. Original pub. Marietta Ga, 1950.

Bradley, Stephen E., Early records of North Carolina (Secretary of State papers). By author, Keysville VA., 1992,1993 (multi- volume)

Broughton, Carrie, L., Marriage and Death Notices in Raleigh Register and North Carolina State Gazette 1799-1825. GPC, Baltimore, 1975.

Camin, Betty J., Surry County North Carolina Estates Index. Published by author, 1991?. This item is in The North Carolina State Library, Raleigh.

Camin, Betty & Edwin, North Carolina Bastardy Bonds. Published by the Authors, Mt Airy NC, 1990.

Campbell, Jeffrey A., Marriages of Rowan County, North Carolina 1762-1850. Closson Press, Apollo PA, 2004. (This work was transcribed from 3 FHL microfilms & is not at all complete.)

Clark, Murtie June, The Pension Roll of 1835, in CD The Revolutionary Pension Lists, Broderbund, 1998.

Clift, G. Glen, "The Second Census of Kentucky, 1800". GPC various reprints 1966 - 2005. Original Frankfort KY, 1954.

Crouch, John, Historical Sketches of Wilkes County, North Carolina. The Chronicle Job Office, Wilkesboro, 1902. Reprint 1979.

DAR, Patriot Index volume III, Gateway Press, 2003

DAR, Roster of Soldiers from North Carolina in the American Revolution. Durham, NC, USA: The North Carolina Daughters of the American Revolution, 1932.

Davidson, Grace Gillam, Early Records of Georgia, 2 vols, 1932. Pub. by Rev. Silas Lucas jr., Vidalia Ga. In 1968.

De Lamar, Marie & Elizabeth Rothstein, The Reconstructed 1790 Census of Georgia. GPC, Baltimore, 1985.

Dorrel, Ruth & Thomas D. Hamm, Abstracts of the Records of the Society of Friends in Indiana. Vol 1, revised, Indiana Historical Society, 1996.

Guilford County Genealogical Society, Abstracts of Marriage Bonds & Additional Data, Guilford County 1771-1840. 1981 .

Grigg, Barbara N., Deed Abstracts Randolph County Books 1-5, 1779-1794. By author, no date. Available NCDAH, Raleigh.

Grigg, Barbara N. & Carolyn N. Hager, 1820 Tax List, Randolph County North Carolina. Randolph County Historical Society, Asheboro, 1978.

Grigg, Barbara N., Carolyn N. Hager, & Albert B. Pruitt, Randolph County NC Land entries, 1779, 1780 & 1783-1801.

Gwynn, Zae Hargett, Court Minutes of Granville County North Carolina, 1746-1820. J.W. Watson, Rocky Mount NC, 1977.

Hatcher, Patricia Law, Abstract of graves of revolutionary patriots, Vol 4, S-Z. (Isaac Wellborn, p172.) Heritage Books, Westminster, MD. 2007 ed.

Haun, Weynette P., North Carolina Revolutionary Army Accounts; Secretary of State Treasurer's & Comptollers Papers. By author?, Durham NC, 1990.

Heinemann, Chas B., First Census of Kentucky. G. Brumbaugh reprints; GPC 1993. (Original 1940).

Hickerson, Thomas F., Happy Valley (The Yadkin Valley) History & Genealogy. by author, Chapel Hill NC, 1940.

Hinshaw, Winford C., 1815 Tax List of Randolph County, N. C.. WPJ Genealogical Publications, Raleigh 1957.

Hofmann, Margaret M., The Province of North Carolina Abstracts of Land Patents, 1663-1729, by author, Roanoke Rapids, 1979.

--------------------, The Colony of North Carolina 1735-1764 Abstracts of Land Patents, v 1, by author, 1982.

--------------------, The Colony of North Carolina 1765-1775 Abstracts of Land Patents, v 2, by author, 1984.

--------------------, The Granville District of North Carolina, 1748-1763, Abstracts of Grants, vol 2. by Author, Waldon NC , The Roanoke News, 1987.
(Granville, Orange), vol 3 (Rowan)

Holcomb, Brent H. comp., Marriages of Granville County, North Carolina. Clearfield, Baltimore, MD., 1997.

--------------------, comp., Marriages of Surry County, North Carolina, 1779-1868. Clearfield, Baltimore, MD., 1998.

--------------------, comp., Marriages of Wilkes County, North Carolina, 1778-1868. Clearfield, Baltimore, MD., 1998.

--------------------, South Carolina Royal Grants, vol 4, Grant Books 25-31, 1772-1775. SCMAR, Columbia, 2009.

Hudson, Frank P., A 1790 Census for Wilkes County, Georgia Prepared from Tax Returns etc. The Reprint Co., Spartanburg SC, 1988.

Hughes, Fred, Guilford County, N.C.; a map supplement. The Custom House, Jamestown N.C., 1988. (The map locates property in each land-holders name. The accompanying booklet does not indicate how these locations were determined.)

Johnson, William Perry, Surry-Wilkes Counties Taxables, 1771-1800. by author, Raleigh 1974.

-------------- Abstrctr, 1779 Randolph Co., NC Tax List. Mountain Press, Signal Mountain, TN, [no date].

King, J.E.S., Early Kentucky Wills. Reprint GPC 1969 (1933).

Kluttz, James W., Abstracts of Deed Books Rowan County, North Carolina. In 5 vols, by author. (This extraordinary series is in the Library of Congress, The State Library of North Carolina, Raleigh.& in The Family History Library, Salt Lake).
  Abstracts of Deed Books 11-14, 1786-1797, pub Landis NC, 1996.
  Abstracts of Deed Books 15-19, 1797-1807, pub Cary NC, 1997.
  Abstracts of Deed Books 20-24, 1807-1818, pub Cary NC, 1999.

Knight, Lucian L., Georgia's Roster in the Revolution. Georgia Dept. Archives & Hist. GPC, 1967.

Leary, Helen F. M., ed., North Carolina Research. 2nd ed., N.C. Genealogical Society, Raleigh, 1996.

Leach, M. S., Record Book (Necrology). Duke University microfilm, fide Charles White. RCGJ VII(3), 1983. (Notes on this unusual volume are included in the article. Little is known about the Book, apparently originating in the Leach family c1859.) Deaths included: William Wellborn 26 June 1832; John Wellborn Dec 15 1830; others ~1875.

Leffel, John C., ed. History of Posey County (IN), Standard Pub. Co., Chicago, 1913.

Linn, Jo White, Rowan County North Carolina Abstracts of the Minutes of the Court of Pleas & Quarter Sessions, 1753-1762 (& also 1762-1774, 1775-1789) 3 vols. Pub. By author, Salisbury, 1977, 1982.

----------------, Abstracts of the Minutes of The Court of Common Pleas and Quarter Sessions, vol 2, pub by author, 1977, p125.

----------------, Abstracts of Wills & Estate Records of Rowan County, 1753-1805 and Tax Lists 1759 & 1778. By author, Salisbury, 1980.

----------------, Lists of Taxables in Rowan County, 1768, Abstract of the Minutes of the Court of Pleas & Quarter Sessions, 1774, v II, p198.

----------------, Rowan County Deed Abstracts, vol 1 1762-1772; vol 2 1753-1762. Pub. By author, typescript, no date. (Available Clayton Library, Houston TX.)

----------------, Surry County, North Carolina Wills 1771-1827. GPC., Baltimore, 1992. Annotated genealogical abstracts.

----------------, 1815 Rowan County, North Carolina Tax List. By author, Salisbury, NC, 1987.

----------------, Rowan County Deed Abstracts, vol 1 1762-1772; Pub. by author, 1983, p111. The abstract is from Deed Book 7: folio 357 (July 1771).

----------------, Abstracts of the Court of Common Pleas and Quarter Sessions, vol 2, pub by author, 1977, p125.

Lucas, Rev. Silas, jr. Some Colonial Georgia Records. In 4 vols, Southern Historical Press, Easley SC, 1977-1991.

--------------------, Index to Headrights & Bounty Grants, Georgia 1756- 1909. Georgia Genealogical Reprints. Vidalia ?? 1970.

McBride, Ransom & Janet McBride, Divorces & Separations from Petitions to the North Carolina General Assembly, 1779-1837. Pub ?. [The full text of this petition is from The General Assembly Special Records, #523, p 180, 1823-1824.]

McCall, Mrs Howard H. comp., Roster of Revolutionary Soldiers in Georgia, vol 1. Clearfield Reprints (GPC), 1996 (Original 1941)

Mayhill, R. Thomas, Land Entry Atlas of Henry County Indiana, 1821-1849. The Bookmark, Knightstown, 1980. Large 10x13", unpaged.

Miller, Alan N., East Tennessee's forgotten children: apprentices from 1778 to 1911. Clearfield, Baltimore, 2000.

Mitchell, Thornton W., North Carolina Wills: A Testator Index,1665-1900. Corrected & revised edition, GPC, Baltimore, 1993.

Moore, John W., History of North Carolina; from earliest discoveries to the present time. Vol II. Raleigh: Alfred Williams & CO, 1880.

Moss, Bobby G., Roster of South Carolina Patriots in the American Revolution. GPC., Baltimore, 1983.

National Association of the Daughters of the American Revolution, DAR Patriot Index, 3 vols., Gateway Press, Baltimore ,2003.

North Carolina Daughters of the American Union. Roster of Soldiers from North Carolina in the American Revolution. GPC, 2007. (Original Durham, 1932.)

Osbourne, Adlai, List of Taxable Properties in the County of Rowan, North Carolina, 1778. Accessed Ancestry.com.

Peden, E. C., comp., Barren County Kentucky Will Book No. 1. C.H. Peden, pub., Glasgow KY, 1979   (P33)

Pruitt, A. B., Abstracts of Land Entries. Holdings by County. (Rowan Co 1778-1795.)   By author, 1987, available LOC.

Register, Alvaretta, K., State Census of North Carolina. 2nd ed. revised, GPC 1971.

Register, Kentucky Historical Society, GPC 1984.

Ratcliff, Clarence E., North Carolina Taxpayers, 2 vols. GPC, 1987-1989.

Reeves, Henry A., Cemetery Inscriptions, Davidson (Old Rowan County) North Carolina. By author, typescript, c1970. (Available Asheboro NC Public Library.)

Reeves, Henry & Mary J. Davis Shoaf, comps. Davidson County, North Carolina Will Summaries. By authors, Lexington NC, c1979.

Robertson, James R., Petitions of Early Inhabitants of Kentucky. Reprint of 1914 edition, Southern Historical Press, *Easly*, 1981.

Rumple, Rev. Jethro, A History of Rowan County North Carolina. J.J. Bruner, Salisbury NC 1881. Reprint

Shields, Ruth H., Abstracts of wills recorded in Orange County, North Carolina, 1752-1800 and Abstracts of wills recorded in Orange County, North Carolina, 1800-1850 (and 202 marriages not shown in Orange County marriage bonds). GPC, Baltimore, 1972.

Shoaf, Mary Jo Davis, Davidson County North Carolina Abstracts of Wills, Book 2, 1844-1868, & Deed Book 3 1826-1828. Pub by author, Roanoke VA, 1989.

Sistler, Byron & Barbara Sistler, Index to Early Tennessee Tax Lists. Pub. By authors, Evanston IL, 1977.

Smith, Sarah Quinn, Early Georgia Wills & Settlements of Estates; Wilkes County. Clearfield Pub., 2003 (1959)

Stewart, William C. Comp., 1800 Census of Pendleton District South Carolina. National Genealogical Society, undated.

Sutherland, James F., Early Kentucky Landholders, 1787-1811. GPC 1986.

Texas Society of the DAR, The Roster of Texas Daughters of Revolutionary Ancestors, vol. 4, 1976. Where?

Thompson, Ruth F. & Louice J. Hartgrove, Abstracts of Marriage Bonds & Additional Data, Guilford County, 1771-1840. Guilford County Genealogical Society, Pub. III, 1981.

Turner, Grace & Miles S. Philbeck, comps, Wilkes County North Carolina Will Abstracts, 1777-1910. By authors, Wilson Co., NC, 1988. (This very good compilation is difficult to find- The Library of Congress has a copy.)

Marriage and Death Notices from the Western Carolinian (Salisbury, North Carolina) 1820-1842. Robert M. Topkins, comp., The Reprint Co., Spartansburg, SC, 1983 (The original 1975)

Waters, Margaret R., Indiana Land Entries, vol 2, part 1, Vincennes Dist.1807-1877. Reprint of the 1948 original. The Bookmark, Knightstown 1980.

Webster, Irene B. comp., Guilford County (NC) Will Abstracts, 1771-1841. By author, 1979.

Weeks, Eve B., trans, Register of Orange County, North Carolina Deeds- 1752-1768 & 1793. Heritage Papers, Danielsville GA, 1984.

Welborn, Gene, Welborns and related families with roots in North and South Carolina. By author, Greenwood SC,1994.

Wheeler, John, H., Historical Sketches of North Carolina, 1584-1851. GPC (Clearfield) 1993 (1825).

White, Virgil D., Genealogical Abstracts of the Revolutionary War Pension Files, Vol III. National Historical Publishing Co., Waynesboro TN, 1992.

———   , Index to the War of 1812 Pension Files, vol III. National Historical Publishing Co., Waynesboro TN, 1989.

Wilburn, Hiram C., Welborn-Wilburn History, Genealogy. Micro-reproduction of the original published Waynesville N.C. Miller Printing, Asheville, 1953. Available FHL film 1421486.

Willie, Betty, Pendleton District South Carolina Deeds, 1790-1806. Southern Historical Press, Easley SC, 1982.

Wilder, Minnie S., comp., Kentucky Soldiers of the War of 1812, Clearfield reprint, original 1931.

Wooley, James E., Ed., A Collection of Upper South Carolina Genealogical and Family Reords, v 1, Southern Historical Press, Easley SC, 1979, p335.

APPENDIX THREE
Petitions & Tax

DATE	COUNTY	P, T	SOURCE {for formal sources see Appendix Two}
1759	Rowan	T?	JWL, Abs of Wills, Estates.
1761	Rowan	T	NCDAH CR85.701.1
1768	Rowan	T	NCGSJ IX(4) 39-46.
1768	Orange	P	Colonial Recs NC v7, p810 RecsExecCouncil, p611.
1771	Orange/Guilford	P	MARSid 308.11.2 + 308.11.1.2.1
1771	Guilford	P	RecsExecCouncil, p678 Regulator pardon Colonial Recs of NC v9, pps 23-26.
1773	Guilford	P	RCGJ X, pps33-37 Courthouse location
1775	Surry/Wilkes	T	Wm P Johnson, Surry-Wilkes Taxable,1974.
1775/6	Rowan	T	NCGS 1(1) Feb 82, p46.
1778 #133.	Rowan	T	A.W.Burns (Osborne), JWL, Deed Abs v2
1778	Granville Dist.	O	Colonial Recs of NC v22, p179. Oaths
1779	Randolph	T	RCGJ XXIV(1), p24 + WP Johnson.
1779	Guilford	P	NCGSJ 38(2), p140-141. For new County
1785 location	Randolph	P	RCGJ III(1), pps 29-39. Courthouse
1785	Randolph	T	RCGJ II(1,2), pps 36ff.

1785	Surry	T	In Surry County NC Wills, JWL p120.
1788	Randolph	P	RCGJ III(1), pps 29-39, Courthouse location.
1792	Rowan	P	RCREG 13(1), p2908.
1799	Rowan	P	RCREG 14(1).
1803	Randolph	T	RCGJ xi(1) 1987, p 3-6.
1813	Randolph	T	RCGJ IX(2), p5ff.
1815	Randolph	T	W.C. Hinshaw. census substitute
1815	Rowan	T	JWLinn, pvt pub.
1820	Randolph	T	RCHS, Grigg&Hager, p17 census substitute.

www.ingramcontent.com/pod-product-compliance
Lightning Source LLC
Chambersburg PA
CBHW070907270326
41927CB00011B/2482